WARRIOR NOTES

including
- *Life and Background of the Author*
- *Introduction to the Work*
- *A Brief Synopsis*
- *List of Characters*
- *Genealogy*
- *Critical Commentaries*
- *Critical Essays*
- *Review Questions and Essay Topics*
- *Selected Bibliography*

by
Soon-Leng Chua, M.A.
University of Illinois
and
Margaret Poh Choo Chua, B.A.
Australian National University

INCORPORATED
LINCOLN, NEBRASKA 68501

Editor

Gary Carey, M.A.
University of Colorado

Consulting Editor

James L. Roberts, Ph.D.
Department of English
University of Nebraska

ISBN 0-8220-1381-9
© Copyright 1998
by
Cliffs Notes, Inc.
All Rights Reserved
Printed in U.S.A.

1998 Printing

The Cliffs Notes logo, the names "Cliffs" and "Cliffs Notes," and the black and yellow diagonal-stripe cover design are all registered trademarks belonging to Cliffs Notes, Inc., and may not be used in whole or in part without written permission.

Cliffs Notes, Inc.   Lincoln, Nebraska

CONTENTS

Life and Background of the Author 5

Introduction to the Work 7

A Brief Synopsis 9

List of Characters 10

Critical Commentaries
    "No Name Woman" 12
    "White Tigers" 23
    "Shaman" 37
    "At the Western Palace" 54
    "A Song for a Barbarian Reed Pipe" 67

Critical Essays
    The Theme of the Voiceless Woman
        in *The Woman Warrior* 81
    The Woman Warrior in Its Historical Context 84
    The Woman Warrior in the Chinese Literary Context ... 87

Review Questions and Essay Topics 90

Selected Bibliography 94

    Center Spread: *The Woman Warrior* / *China Men* Genealogy

THE WOMAN WARRIOR

Notes

LIFE AND BACKGROUND OF THE AUTHOR

Maxine Hong Kingston, an eminent memoirist and a celebrated Chinese-American autobiographer, is best known for *The Woman Warrior: Memoirs of a Girlhood Among Ghosts* (1976) and its companion volume, *China Men* (1980). *The Woman Warrior* won the National Book Critics Circle Award in 1976 for non-fiction, and *China Men* was awarded the 1980 American Book Award. Kingston's unusual blend of fantasy, autobiography, and Chinese folklore makes her works highly personal and unconventional. *The Woman Warrior* and *China Men* are heavily influenced by many related sources, particularly her mother's childhood stories of China, her own experiences as a first-generation Chinese American, the less-than-favorable treatment of her ancestors who immigrated to America, and the racism and denigration of women that she encountered growing up in post-World War II California.

Maxine Ting Ting Hong was born on October 27, 1940, in Stockton, California, which had been a major supply center during the California gold-rush era of the mid nineteenth century. A year earlier, in 1939, her mother, Ying Lan Hong, had arrived from China at Ellis Island, New York, to join her husband, Tom, who had emigrated from China to the United States fifteen years earlier. Named for a blond female gambler whom her father had met while working in a gambling establishment in California, Maxine, the first of six American-born children in the family, grew up in Stockton's Chinatown, where her parents owned a laundry business. She never felt that her parents encouraged her to do well in her academic studies, in part because in their conservative Chinese culture, women often were not expected to have careers outside of the home. Her negative childhood experiences are reflected in *The Woman Warrior*, in which she exhibits a certain bitterness leveled at her parents, as well as at American and Chinese cultures.

After having excelled in her high-school studies, Hong won eleven scholarships that allowed her to attend the University of California at Berkeley, from which she graduated in 1962. That same year, she married Earll Kingston, an actor. Two years later, she returned to Berkeley to pursue a teaching certificate, which she received in 1965. For the next two years, she taught English and mathematics in Hayward, California, and then in 1967, she, her husband, and their son, Joseph, moved to the island of Hawaii, where her great-grandfathers first had worked when they immigrated to America. In *China Men*, Kingston describes the experiences of her forefathers working on the rough plantations of Hawaii, which they called Sandalwood Mountains.

In Hawaii, Kingston taught English at the state university and at Mid-Pacific Institute, a private school; in her spare time, she wrote. When *The Woman Warrior* was published in 1976 and became an immediate and unqualified success, she retired from teaching and devoted her energies to writing. *China Men*, which relates the ordeals of the male members of Kingston's family in America, appeared in 1980, followed by *Hawaii One Summer* (1987), a collection of twelve prose selections. In 1989, she published *Tripmaster Monkey: His Fake Book*, her first traditionally structured novel, in which she tells the fictitious story of Whitman Ah Sing, a Chinese American living in Berkeley, California, during the counter-culture 1960s, with its hippies, tie-dyed tee-shirts, and drug addiction. The energetic adventures of Whitman Ah Sing, whose name evokes images of the American poet Walt Whitman and his refrain phrase "I sing"—"Ah Sing"—reveal the protagonist's unease about his role and future in America.

Kingston is a frequent commentator and guest speaker at academic conferences and cultural events across the country, and she has often found it necessary to write articles defending *The Woman Warrior*, explaining herself and rebutting some critics who feel that the famous autobiography focuses too much on exotic Chinese history and not enough on the day-to-day racism that Chinese Americans face in American society. To these charges, Kingston responds that she is not trying to represent Chinese culture; she is portraying her *own* experiences.

INTRODUCTION TO THE WORK

The Woman Warrior, a work that defies easy classification, is neither wholly a work of fiction nor, strictly speaking, an autobiography. A clever blend of fantasy, childhood memories, folklore, and family history, Kingston's work is revolutionary precisely because it transcends genres. Her unique literary skills, vision, and style have established her as one of the most significant American writers in the late twentieth century. Simultaneously a historical, fictional, biographical, and imaginative work, *The Woman Warrior* is studied not only in English literature classes but also in anthropology, women's studies, sociology, folklore, and American and ethnic studies, as well as history.

Two reasons why *The Woman Warrior* is hard to label are its lack of a strictly linear plot, with each chapter's story self-contained and independent of other chapters, and its content, which seems so different from traditional memoirs. While many American autobiographical works, such as *The Autobiography of Benjamin Franklin* and *The Autobiography of Malcolm X*, detail the struggles of their protagonists, who generally rise from a low status in society to achieve success, *The Woman Warrior* works differently. Kingston provides scant information about her post-college adult life and her successful career as a teacher. Absent from *The Woman Warrior* is a conspicuous and clearly defined episode of reaching a successful stage in life—be it financial, religious, or otherwise—typically seen in many other American autobiographies. Instead, Kingston presents the *writing* of her autobiography itself as her success, her cathartic act of making peace with her family and society, and gaining an understanding of herself, of who she is and where she fits in the world around her. Readers who expect a story about achieving success as defined by standard American mythology—the American Dream—sometimes find *The Woman Warrior* disappointing.

For her part, Kingston considers *The Woman Warrior* very much an autobiography in the American literary tradition. In a 1987 interview with Paula Rabinowitz, in which she discusses both *The Woman Warrior* and *China Men*, Kingston states: "I am trying to write an American language that has Chinese accents. . . . I was claiming the English language and the literature to tell our story as Americans. That is why the forms of the two books are not exactly like other books, and the language and the rhythms are not like other writers, and yet, it's American English."

Ultimately, because of the postmodern, or consciously fragmented, nature of *The Woman Warrior*, Kingston's highly personal autobiography is very Western in character. She is intensely aware that her autobiography is very subjective and that she can present only *her* version of events, not a version officially sanctioned or approved by the entire Chinese-American community. As such, *The Woman Warrior* can be considered a postmodern work because of its self-awareness of presenting only one interpretation of truth, which is a tenet of the postmodern literary movement. For example, at the beginning of the memoir's last chapter, "A Song for a Barbarian Reed Pipe," Kingston confesses that her version of events is often her own interpretation of what she has heard from someone else and not what she has experienced firsthand. She suggests a parallel between herself and the legendary Chinese "knot-makers" who "tied string into buttons and frogs, and rope into bell pulls. There was one knot so complicated that it blinded the knot-maker. Finally an emperor outlawed this cruel knot, and the nobles could not order it anymore. If I had lived in China, I would have been an outlaw knot-maker." Her life's story is like a knot so complicated that it can never be untied and laid out in a straight line.

Whereas other autobiographers tend to present their life stories as factual, Kingston undermines her own authority as narrator, stressing her subjectivity. She provokes readers into stepping back from the text to reflect upon some deeper implication, or subtext. For example, unlike the other chapters, "At the Western Palace" is written in the third-person, and, given commonly held assumptions concerning the nature of autobiography, or "memoirs," as *The Woman Warrior*'s complete title suggests, we would assume that the chapter objectively recounts reality. However, by declaring at the beginning of the next chapter that she personally did not witness the events in "At the Western Palace," Kingston betrays her own subjectivity. Details described in "At the Western Palace" are of Kingston's own making, designed to illustrate her own agenda and to reveal an underlying truth: Autobiography is as much imagined and fictional as it is factual. Kingston's memoir, so intensely aware of itself and its limitations, is filled with a subjectivity that is the hallmark of a postmodernist text.

A BRIEF SYNOPSIS

Divided into five chapters, each of which is more or less self-contained, Maxine Hong Kingston's *The Woman Warrior* explores the many forms of adversity that women face. Kingston uses women's stories to explore her own cultural history. As a first-generation Chinese American, she struggles to reconcile her Chinese cultural heritage with her emerging sense of herself as an American.

In the memoir's first chapter, "No Name Woman," Kingston's mother, Brave Orchid, tells her daughter about an aunt on Kingston's father's side of the family. This aunt, whom Kingston names No Name Woman because her real name is never spoken by the family, becomes pregnant while her husband is working in America. When No Name Woman, who remained behind in China when her husband sought work in America, no longer can hide her pregnancy from her family and her village, the villagers destroy the family home as punishment for her adultery. After giving birth in a pigsty, she kills herself and the baby by drowning in the family well.

In the second chapter, "White Tigers," Kingston recalls the legend of Fa Mu Lan, a woman warrior who leads her people to victory in battle. As a child, Kingston felt girls could not achieve greatness in a man's world. "White Tigers" is the story of her own childhood fantasy of overcoming feelings of inferiority as a female. Like Fa Mu Lan, she imagines herself leaving home at seven years of age and being brought up by martial arts teachers. She becomes a great warrior, triumphantly returning to her home to save her people.

"Shaman" relates the story of Brave Orchid's extraordinary medical career as a midwife in China. After giving birth to two children in China, Brave Orchid takes the unusual step of attending medical school, after which she works as a doctor in her home village and becomes a very successful healer. Eventually, she gives up her career to join her husband in America. However, unable to practice medicine in America, she and her husband open a laundry business in California.

As *The Woman Warrior* progresses, Kingston relies less on her mother's narratives and more on her own recollections of family events and of experiences growing up. In the memoir's fourth chapter, "At the Western Palace," she writes about her aunt, Moon Orchid, who fails to assimilate into American culture. Moon Orchid's husband arrived alone in America and became a successful doctor. However, after many years of practicing medicine in Los Angeles, he remarried and abandoned Moon Orchid, who remained in Hong Kong waiting for him to send for her. Brave Orchid, determined to have Moon Orchid confront this irresponsible man, arranges for her sister to immigrate to America, but when Moon Orchid finally faces her husband, he again rejects her and chides her for disrupting his life and career. Moon Orchid subsequently goes mad, ending her days in an insane asylum.

In the last chapter, "A Song for a Barbarian Reed Pipe," in which Kingston describes her childhood emotional experiences and the conflicts she felt growing up in a Chinese household in America, she depicts the pains of finding a personal identity and a voice to express herself to her parents and a society that do not understand her. She ends *The Woman Warrior* with the legend of Ts'ai Yen, an ancient Chinese female poet who was captured by a non-Chinese tribe and who lived among these nomadic people for twelve years but could never fully assimilate into their culture. Kingston strongly implies that her mother is like Ts'ai Yen in that Brave Orchid longs to return to her Chinese village, but Kingston also suggests that she too sees herself as a foreigner among Americans, caught between the Chinese traditions of her parents and American culture's emphasis on individuality. Her memoir is similar to Ts'ai Yen's cathartic song, which the barbarians cannot understand: "Her words seemed to be Chinese, but the barbarians understood their sadness and anger."

LIST OF CHARACTERS

Maxine

The central character in *The Woman Warrior*. Shy, awkward, introspective, and intellectual, she describes her anguished childhood years and her coming to terms with two competing cultures, American and Chinese.

No Name Woman

Maxine's Chinese aunt, who drowned herself and her baby after villagers ransacked her house as punishment for her extramarital sexual affair with a man who probably forced himself on her. Kingston, who names this aunt "No Name Woman" because her family refuses to mention the aunt's real name ever again, devotes a chapter to her partly to end this silence.

Brave Orchid

Maxine's mother, who attended medical school in China before she joined her husband in America. Her name suggests a brave, resilient, resourceful, and sometimes harsh character.

Moon Orchid

Brave Orchid's sister, whose name implies a delicate, elegant, but passive nature. Unfortunately, her passivity does not help her survive after her husband rejects her when she arrives in America. Brave Orchid ends up in a mental asylum.

Tom

Kingston's father, who came to America and worked in New York for years before sending for his wife in China. In *China Men*, the companion volume to *The Woman Warrior*, we learn that Kingston's father is a gentle and scholarly man who left a teaching career in China to support his family as a laundry worker.

Fa Mu Lan

The legendary Chinese heroine who appears in Chinese ballads, novels, operas, and other literary forms. Historians do not agree on whether or not this Chinese Joan of Arc really existed. As a child, Kingston fantasized about becoming Fa Mu Lan.

Ts'ai Yen

A Chinese historical figure who in 195 was captured by nomads and held captive for twelve years. A scholar, poet, and musician, Ts'ai Yen describes her years of alienation and exile in "Eighteen Stanzas for a Barbarian Reed Pipe," from which Kingston gets the last chapter's title. As an adult, Kingston strongly identifies with Ts'ai Yen.

The Silent Girl

The Chinese girl whom Kingston bullies in sixth grade. Kingston fears that this girl's negative public image implies her own unpopularity and non-conformity.

CRITICAL COMMENTARIES

"NO NAME WOMAN"

Maxine Hong Kingston begins her search for a personal identity with the story of an aunt, to whom this first chapter's title refers. Ironically, the first thing we read is Kingston's mother's warning Kingston, "You must not tell anyone . . . what I am about to tell you. In China your father had a sister who killed herself. She jumped into the family well. We say that your father has all brothers because it is as if she had never been born." Of course, keeping silent is exactly what Kingston is *not* doing. Because she is most concerned with exploring how her Chinese cultural history can be reconciled with her emerging sense of herself as an American, Kingston must uncover just what this Chinese cultural history is, and one way of doing so is by listening to, and then altering, her mother's stories about the family's Chinese past.

Throughout *The Woman Warrior*, Kingston will refer to her mother's historical tales as "talk-stories," culturally based, primarily oral stories whose general purpose is didactic. For example, here in "No Name Woman," Kingston says of her mother, who, we later learn, is named Brave Orchid, "Whenever she had to warn us about life, my mother told stories that ran like this one [about No Name Woman], a story to grow up on. She tested our strength to establish realities." Similar to a folktale, a talk-story often involves the fantastic and fuses realistic events with magical qualities. Because of this realistic-magical aspect, a talk-story can be as confusing to its audience—Kingston and her readers—as it can be inspiring.

Brave Orchid's story of No Name Woman provides one valuable inroad into Kingston's discovering her cultural history. Brave Orchid relates how on the night when Kingston's aunt gave birth to an illegitimate child, the people of the Chinese village in which the aunt and her family lived ransacked the family's house, killed all of their livestock, and destroyed their crops. Shunned by her family, the aunt gave birth in a pigsty, alone. The next morning, Brave Orchid went to gather water from the family's well, where she discovered that No Name Woman had committed suicide by throwing herself and her child down into the well.

Explaining that the aunt had become pregnant by a man whose identity the aunt never disclosed, Brave Orchid also relates that at the time—1924—the aunt's husband was working in America. Due to failing crops and a poor domestic economy, many of the men from the ancestral village in China were forced to leave their farms to seek work, traveling as far as America, which the Chinese nicknamed "Gold Mountain" because the original Chinese immigrants initially perceived it as a bountiful land where a good living could be made working in the gold-mining industry.

Brave Orchid's story about Kingston's aunt is a cautionary tale meant to discourage the young Kingston from engaging in premarital sex; hopefully, the fear of humiliation, ostracism, and death will serve sufficiently as a deterrent for sexual promiscuity. Brave Orchid explains to her daughter about the aunt, "Now that you have started to menstruate, what happened to her could happen to you. Don't humiliate us. . . . The villagers are watchful." Here, Brave Orchid's phrase "The villagers are watchful" transcends time and geography: No Name Woman severely crippled her family's social standing in the Chinese village; similarly, Brave Orchid warns her daughter not to embarrass her family, which was among many others that emigrated from their village in China and settled in Stockton, California. Kingston notes of her mother, "Whenever she had to warn us about life, my mother told stories that ran like this one, a story to grow up on." Brave Orchid uses the "talk-story" of No Name Woman to pass on codes of proper conduct and values to her daughter.

Kingston, however, does not fully understand the story's importance when she first hears it. Because she is confused by its many details, she rewrites Brave Orchid's original tale, creating the impetus for why No Name Woman acts as she does in Brave Orchid's version. Kingston knows that her mother is concerned that she not have premarital sex because her mother directly states that that is the reason for telling the story. But what Kingston does not know, at least not until the memoir's final chapter, is that her mother hopes to strengthen her daughter emotionally and psychologically by giving her a sense of who she is and where she came from. In "No Name Woman," Kingston writes, "Those of us in the first American generations have had to figure out how the invisible world the emigrants built around our childhood fits into solid America." China is "invisible," an intangible place that Kingston only hears about; America is "solid" not only because she physically lives in it but because she interacts daily with other Americans and necessarily wants to fit in. How to reconcile this conflict between these two disparate cultures becomes her thesis, the problem she attempts—and ultimately succeeds—to solve.

The young Kingston has difficulty making sense of her mother's story and fails to receive direct, unambiguous responses to her questions and concerns. Her struggle to understand how knowing the history of her aunt who committed suicide will help her conduct herself properly—according to her mother's traditional Chinese code of beliefs—is reflected in the questions she asks directly to Chinese Americans: "Chinese-Americans, when you try to understand what things in you are Chinese, how do you separate what is peculiar to childhood, to poverty, insanities, one family, your mother who marked your growing with stories, from what is Chinese? What is Chinese tradition and what is the movies?" How, Kingston asks, can she decipher what is real and what is fiction in her mother's stories when her mother herself will not tell her? The larger issue, then, becomes how Kingston will integrate such talk-stories into her own personal life as she grows from childhood to womanhood, and just how relevant these tales of life in China are to a first-generation Chinese American with Chinese-born parents. To her American sensibilities, the stories are confusing because they are based on a Chinese context.

Because her mother's messages are difficult to adopt or apply to her immediate American reality, Kingston, after relating Brave Orchid's telling of No Name Woman's story, rewrites the tale from her own American perspective. She uses her own style of "talk-story" to guess the reasons for her aunt's actions. Ironically, although at the time she probably would not have recognized it, nor perhaps have wanted to, Kingston's rewriting her mother's talk-story as her own indicates an important element in her reconciling her Chinese past and her American present: She learns to talk-story by having listened to her mother. In this way, a continuity is established between her mother, who represents the cultural traditions of China, and herself as a first-generation Chinese American. Kingston will finally acknowledge this succession of generations when, at the end of "Shaman," she compares herself favorably to her mother and proudly recognizes their many similarities: "I am really a Dragon, as she is a Dragon, both of us born in dragon years. I am practically a first daughter of a first daughter."

Kingston rewrites No Name Woman's story based on her own understanding of the patriarchal nature of traditional Chinese society, in which women were conditioned to do as they were told, without question. Because of the close-knit community in which No Name Woman lived, Kingston contends that her aunt's sexual partner "was not a stranger because the village housed no strangers." Ironically, Kingston reasons, the same patriarchal society that subjugated women to subservient roles bears responsibility for No Name Woman's adultery. Because No Name Woman was conditioned to do everything that she was ordered to do, she was unable to gather the personal strength necessary to repel the man's sexual advances. This inability emphasizes what Kingston argues is the great disparity between how women and men were supposed to act: "Women in the old China did not choose. Some man had commanded her to lie with him and be his secret evil. . . . She obeyed him; she always did as she was told." Even more damning of this double standard in "old China" is Kingston's assertion that this man who basically raped No Name Woman was the same villager who organized the raid against No Name Woman's family. Kingston's version of Brave Orchid's original talk-story emphasizes how a dutifully submissive woman is victimized by a man's abusive manipulation of a gender-biased social code.

Kingston also exposes the unfair discrimination against women in traditional Chinese society when she discusses how sons are celebrated more than daughters. She imagines that her aunt's illegitimate child must have been a girl: "It was probably a girl; there is some hope of forgiveness for boys." Only a mad person, as her grandfather is described to have been, would prefer a female child over a male. Sons were venerated because they could pass on the family name, thereby ensuring a family's stability and longevity; in contrast, daughters, who were given away by their parents at marriage, primarily functioned only as bearers of sons for their husbands' families. Such was the traditional code and operation of a patrilineal society that enforced its patriarchal ideology by imposing restrictions on women's positions and conduct. Improper actions, such as No Name Woman's, were considered a breach of this code and could lead to severe consequences, including death. Because Kingston's aunt had an adulterous affair and, even worse, probably produced a *female* child from the sexual union, she threatened what Kingston terms the "roundness"—the harmony and the wholeness—of her family and the larger community. This prized circularity was so enmeshed in everyday life—symbolically, in "the round moon cakes and round doorways, the round tables of graduated sizes that fit one roundness inside another, round windows and rice bowls"—that the slightest ripple, the tiniest threat, to social stability was believed by the villagers to be an outright attack on an entire way of life and therefore must be completely annihilated.

No Name Woman is attacked because her action—adultery, confirmed by pregnancy—threatens socially accepted behavior tacitly enforced through centuries of tradition. "In the village structure," Kingston notes, "spirits shimmered among the live creatures, balanced and held in equilibrium by time and land." When No Name Woman's family banishes her from the family, she runs out into the fields surrounding the house and falls to the ground, "her own land no more." Her family no longer considers her among the "live creatures, balanced and held in equilibrium by time and land." What these shimmering "spirits" are is not entirely clear, but their presence implies that both the living and the nonliving actively and forcefully protect the many traditions that stabilize the society. In No Name Woman's case, her illegitimate child violates the immense value placed on a traditional family and is, for the family, another mouth to feed. Ironically, the aunt's and her child's fates are almost whimsically determined by the time in which these actions take place; Kingston surmises, "If my aunt had betrayed the family at a time of large grain yields and peace, when many boys were born, and wings were being built on many houses, perhaps she might have escaped such severe punishment. . . . Adultery, perhaps only a mistake during the good times, became a crime when the village needed food." Remember, too, that we are told that the aunt had returned from her husband's family to live with her own. Perhaps she was thrown out because she was another mouth to feed during her husband's absence.

No Name Woman's family is implicated in her "crime" and therefore must suffer the ransacking of their house. According to Chinese custom, because the family was responsible for the daughter's wrongdoing, it should have prevented the adultery in the first place. Kingston's aunt is doubly punished by witnessing her family's being made to suffer. The family knows and must accept that it will be attacked for No Name Woman's transgression of the community's social code of how women should behave, which explains its reported passivity and resignation to the ransacking.

Kingston speculates further that her aunt may have taken some pride in her personal appearance and expressed her individuality. Any such display would have been a contravention to the established proper conduct in which young men and women learned to "efface their sexual color and present plain miens." Perhaps the aunt was seeking some affection or even romance: "She dreamed of a lover for the fifteen days of New Year's. . . . And sure enough she cursed the year, the family, the village, and herself." Traditionally, the Chinese New Year is a fifteen-day celebration beginning either in late January or early February. Because people's actions, activities, and practices during the celebration set the pattern for the entire new year, the new year must begin auspiciously.

Kingston wants to believe that her aunt had at least some positive control of her own destiny rather than being merely a victim. In this less feasible scenario that Kingston feels it necessary to create, her aunt is more than just a victim who is married to a stranger, estranged immediately, raped, then ostracized by her family and community, and finally left with no choice but to commit suicide. Unfortunately, though, Kingston must acknowledge that the aunt killed both herself and her newborn baby, which leaves us very little room to doubt the horrific events contained in Brave Orchid's telling of No Name Woman's story. However, Kingston would like to think—perhaps she finds it emotionally necessary to believe—that Brave Orchid fabricated many of the story's details according to the emphasis that she intended to impress on Kingston.

Although Kingston tries to make sense of what her mother tells her, she remains unsure about the reliability of the facts surrounding her aunt's suicide, as are we. The confusion and ambivalence she feels as the author, who was once the listener, parallel ours. Her mother talked-story orally; she talks-story in print. Brave Orchid may have believed that the story would prevent her daughter from having sexual relations outside marriage and thereby bringing shame upon the family, but the daughter interprets the story according to values that she can relate to—namely, individualism and a strong, nurturing sense of womanhood.

One of the ways that this individualism and womanhood are defined is through language, or, at least for No Name Woman, the lack of it. Overall in the memoir, there is a movement from silence in the first line of the first chapter—"You must not tell anyone"—to language in the last line of the last chapter—"It translated well." For Kingston, silence—the absence of language—equals voicelessness, which in turn means the loss of identity as a woman, a Chinese American, an adult, all of which are what she is trying to find. However, she is very aware of the emotional risks she is taking by asserting her independence from her own Chinese community. When her aunt violated *her* community's standards of acceptable behavior, "the villagers punished her for acting as if she could have a private life, secret and apart from them."

Silence both begins and ends "No Name Woman," which balances Kingston's mother's opening sentence with Kingston's own thoughts about how fearfully powerful silence can be: "The Chinese are always very frightened of the drowned one, whose weeping ghost, wet hair hanging and skin bloated, waits silently by the water to pull down a substitute." Here, Kingston fears for herself: If she remains silent and fails to find her own personal voice, she risks becoming a "substitute" for her aunt, who remained silent her entire life. Unwittingly—perhaps—Kingston's mother increases her daughter's anxiety when she admonishes her never to repeat No Name Woman's story: "Don't tell anyone you had an aunt."

But telling everyone that she had an aunt is *exactly* what Kingston does, and for a very complex reason. If Kingston's purpose in writing *The Woman Warrior* is to solidify her identity as a female Chinese American, then for her to remain silent about her aunt is tantamount to her rejecting her own sense of self. She cannot deny a voice for her aunt—"my aunt, my forerunner"—without denying one for herself, which is why she reinterprets Brave Orchid's talk-story by creating a more individualized life for her aunt, who, she imagines, used a "secret voice, a separate attentiveness," much like she herself does throughout the memoir. "Unless I see her life branching into mine," Kingston writes of No Name Woman, "she gives me no ancestral help."

As with all of the female protagonists in her mother's talk-stories, Kingston's reworking of the No Name Woman tale emphasizes the similarities between her aunt and herself. For example, describing how her aunt "combed individuality" into her hair, Kingston imagines that first she "brushed her hair back from her forehead," then "looped a piece of thread, knotted into a circle between her index fingers and thumbs," around any loose hairs across her front hairline, and finally "pulled the thread away from her skin, ripping the hairs out neatly." Significantly, Kingston then writes, "My mother did the same to me and my sisters and herself," which draws a parallel between her aunt and herself. Even more important in this ritual of how No Name Woman pulls out any loose hairs are the shadows of her hands, which Kingston describes as "a pair of shadow geese biting." The making of this complicated knot foreshadows the last chapter, "A Song for a Barbarian Reed Pipe," in which Kingston relates the story of ancient Chinese knot-makers, who tied string into intricate designs, one of which was so complicated that it blinded the knot-maker. "If I had lived in China," Kingston speculates, "I would have been an outlaw knot-maker," which is an indirect reference to No Name Woman.

Although Kingston honors her aunt by retelling No Name Woman's story in *The Woman Warrior*, she blames herself for having kept silent about this woman for more than twenty years. She writes, "But there is more to this silence: they want me to participate in her punishment. And I have." Here, the short sentence "And I have" emphasizes the guilt Kingston still feels for having neglected No Name Woman's memory for as long as she has. Having told a family secret, she fears recrimination from her parents and, ironically, worries that her aunt haunts her because she is displeased that Kingston has revealed her story. "I do not think she always means me well," Kingston writes about her aunt. "I am telling on her, and she was a spite suicide, drowning herself in the [family] drinking water." However, Kingston also reveals that it was necessary, both for her own sense of self and to honor her aunt's memory, to countermand Brave Orchid's wish that she keep No Name Woman's story a secret: "The [aunt's] real punishment was not the raid swiftly inflicted by the villagers, but the family's deliberately forgetting her. Her betrayal so maddened them, they saw to it that she would suffer forever, even after death." Although Kingston never learns what her aunt's real name is, she alleviates her ancestor's long suffering by giving her the only name she can: No Name Woman.

(Here and in the following chapters, difficult words, allusions, and phrases are explained.)

- **contracts** labor contracts, specifying the length and wages of work; by 1924, when Kingston's male relatives left China to work in other countries, the United States had severely limited the number of male Chinese emigrants allowed into the country. Only men who met a strict set of criteria were allowed to enter, but their wives, sons, and daughters were not allowed to come with them.

- **Bali** an Indonesian island, approximately 1500 miles southeast of Vietnam and directly east of Java; during the early twentieth century, Chinese emigrants on Bali probably worked mainly for Dutch-owned private plantations.

- **bunds** here, low walls of dirt, used to enclose water in which rice is grown.

- **loom** a hand-operated apparatus used to weave cloth.

- **earthenware jugs** containers made from either clay or heavy soil; once the material is sculpted into form, the container is cooked over flames and then set to cool.

- **acrid** foul-smelling.

- **birth in the pigsty** Giving birth in a pigsty reflects the superstitious belief that if a mother gives birth in a house and is proud of her baby, evil or envious gods might take the child from its mother; frequently, newborn babies were called pigs to trick the gods into thinking that the babies were ugly or deformed and, therefore, not worth stealing.

- ***Oh, You Beautiful Doll*** a 1949 musical film about a songwriter who whimsically rewrites a serious composer's songs as popular tunes; Betty Grable did not appear in the film as Kingston mistakenly suggests.

- **Betty Grable**   (1916–73) An American actress and film star, she was the most popular pin-up girl of World War II; she costarred with Ginger Rogers and Fred Astaire in *The Gay Divorcee* (1934) and later appeared in such films as *The Pin-up Girl* (1944) and *Moon Over Miami* (1941).

- *She Wore a Yellow Ribbon*   Directed by the legendary John Ford, this 1949 Western film starred John Wayne in one of his greatest performances, as a cavalry commander who delays his retirement because of an impending war with Apaches.

- **John Wayne**   (1907–79) American actor known for his ruggedness as a self-styled individualist in Western films.

- **gizzard lining**   refers to the thickly lined gizzard, found mainly in birds; located directly behind the stomach, the gizzard holds ingested gravel or some other grit-like material that birds must use to digest their food.

- **prodigal**   wastefully extravagant.

- **tractably**   easily led; malleable.

- **proxy**   a stand-in, or substitute; although the rooster that No Name Woman's soon-to-be husband sends to her is intended to be a goodwill gesture, that he sends a rooster rather than meeting her himself indicates traditional China's low regard for women.

- **commensal tradition**   a way of life in which one group of people gains something from another, unaffected group of people; Kingston condemns how Chinese families punish wrongdoers by treating the offenders as pariahs, forced to eat leftovers at an "outcast table."

- **samurais**   Ancient Japanese warriors, the samurais originated in eleventh-century Japan to enforce the laws of the imperial government, whose power was waning; their cultural dominance ended around 1700.

- **geishas**   a Japanese class of indentured women who entertain men; usually, a young girl is sold by her parents to a geisha organization, which then trains her in the duties of being a geisha.

- **synonym**   a word that has the same, or similar, meaning as another word; Kingston writes that in China, marriage is synonymous to "taking a daughter-in-law" because after the wedding, the husband and wife live with his family, never with hers.

- **blunt-cut**   to cut hair to an even, sharply defined length around the entire head; the term "blunt-cut" implies a woman's de-feminizing her appearance.

- **bob**   a short-clipped haircut.

- **shadow geese**   refers to the art of contorting the hands to form different shapes, usually animals, which appear as shadows on a wall or other flat surfaces when the hands are illuminated from behind.

- **depilatory**   hair-removing.

- **to have our feet bound**   Beginning during the T'ang dynasty (618–906), foot-binding was an accepted cultural practice in which a female's feet were severely constricted to retard normal growth. Parents wrapped their daughters' feet with toes extended downward, stretching the instep and inhibiting the shaping of the arch. Although foot-binding was a socially elite practice that signaled a man's wealth and social position because he could afford for his wives and daughters not to work, the female's feet would become so deformed that the woman no longer could walk without being physically supported by servants. This inhumane custom ended in 1911, when the dynastic form of government was replaced with a republic.

- **almanac**   typically, an annual reference book used to predict the future; predictions are based on the positions and movements of the stars and the planets.

- **peroxide**   a chemical solution used as a disinfectant to kill germs.

- **whorls**   spirals; Kingston compares women who carried many objects on their backs to snails and their coiled shells.

- **greatcoat**   an overcoat.

- **efface**   to erase or eliminate.

- **miens**   appearances.

- **pigeon-toed**   feet turned inward, in the shape of an inverted "V."

- **incest**   sex between blood-related kin.

- **atavism**   characteristics that reappear over time; Kingston likens herself to her aunt, No Name Woman: Both women share "an atavism deeper than fear," an unnameable anxiety about relationships with men.

- **brides' prices**   payments made to brides' families by grooms, as a gesture that brides will be treated well by their husbands.

- **dowries**   any material wealth that brides bring to their husbands at marriage.

- **maelstrom**   an incredibly violent and threatening storm, or situation.

- **moon cakes**   round pastries eaten during full moon of the eighth month of the lunar year.
- **talismans**   objects believed to hold magical powers; for example, a person who carries a rabbit's foot will be lucky.
- **fatalism**   a belief system whose adherents believe that all events are predetermined; a person cannot make personal choices because free will does not exist.
- **culpability**   deserving of blame; guiltiness.
- **gall**   generally, resentment, or bitterness; because No Name Woman unknowingly goes into labor immediately after her family disowns her and kicks her out of the house, she fears that the pain racking her body is physically caused by her family's throwing her out.
- **agoraphobia**   a fear of open spaces or public places.
- **flayed**   here, stripped of all protective emotions; left completely vulnerable.
- **spirit money**   fake money that a deceased person's relatives burn to bribe the gods not to harass the deceased person's spirit.
- **incense**   here, a pleasant odor.
- **Chairman Mao**   Mao Zedong (1893–1976), founder of the Chinese Communist Party (1921) and the first chairman (1949–1959) of the People's Republic of China; even after his retirement as chairman, he retained control of the Chinese Communist Party, which in turn controls the country.
- **origamied**   from the Japanese art of origami, which entails folding paper into different shapes without cutting or using adhesives.

"WHITE TIGERS"

Having reclaimed the discarded memory of her aunt by telling her story in "No Name Woman," Kingston continues her search for a Chinese-American identity in a more assertive and positive tone in "White Tigers," which relates the heroic struggle of Fa Mu Lan, one of the women warriors from whom the memoir gets its title.

Whereas the previous chapter begins with an entreaty for silence, "White Tigers" confidently proclaims that many successes are possible for women and, more specifically, for "Chinese girls." Prominent among the many talk-stories Kingston heard while growing up is one involving a woman warrior accomplished in martial arts, a story that Kingston narrates in the chapter's first paragraph as a segue between No Name Woman's history and the tale of Fa Mu Lan. The description of this woman's "combing her hair one morning" recalls how Kingston wanted to believe that No Name Woman "combed individuality into her bob." Also, the comment, "Perhaps women were once so dangerous that they had to have their feet bound," evokes the implied threat in Kingston's mother's telling her daughters that they should be glad that they were not forced to have their feet bound when they were seven years old, and foreshadows the later incident in "White Tigers" when an evil baron's wives, once freed from the cruelly inhumane bandages used to wrap their feet, become fierce women warriors themselves.

For most of this chapter, Kingston relates the talk-story of Fa Mu Lan, the woman-warrior heroine about whom she learned as a child. She blends aspects of the Chinese legend of Fa Mu Lan with other myths stemming from Eastern philosophy and religion. Some of the talk-story's images that appear most extraordinary or fanciful, such as people and swords flying through the air, are based on Chinese popular culture and folklore; Kingston saw these images depicted in Chinese movies while she was growing up in Stockton, California.

Kingston's talk-story about Fa Mu Lan is derived from a classical Chinese folk story about a woman named Mu-lan. Anonymously written in the fifth or sixth century by a Chinese poet, "The Ballad of Mu-lan" sketchily details how Mu-lan, about whose deeds many different versions have since been composed, fights in place of her father when he is drafted into the emperor's army. After the war ends, Mu-lan returns home to her family and resumes her normal life.

The scarcity of detail in the many versions of Mu-lan's story is markedly different from Kingston's revision of the tale. For example, one version of "The Ballad of Mu-lan" begins with the folk heroine volunteering to fight in place of her father, whereas Kingston details Fa Mu Lan's education as a woman warrior; Fa Mu Lan has an older brother who replaces his father in the first round of army conscription, but Mu-lan has no older brother so she must go in place of her father when the army first drafts him; and Kingston's woman warrior fights *against* the emperor, but Mu-lan fights *for* him.

The greatest similarity between Mu-lan and Kingston's Fa Mu Lan is that each heroine returns home after fighting and assumes her traditionally female duties. In one version of "The Ballad of Mu-lan," when the folk heroine, who is weaving at the beginning of the poem, comes home from fighting, the first thing she does is remove her "wartime gown" and put her "old-time clothes" back on, an act that symbolizes that she will resume her duties as a daughter in the household. In Kingston's talk-story, in which Fa Mu Lan marries and has a son, the woman warrior conforms to Chinese custom by going to live with her husband in his family's home. Kneeling at her parents-in-law's feet, she tells them, "I will stay with you, doing farmwork and housework, and giving you more sons."

Whether or not Kingston personally sees herself as Fa Mu Lan has been hotly debated in recent criticism. Is she the woman warrior? Much of the confusion occurs because Kingston initially believes that she first heard the Fa Mu Lan story only after she became an adult, but then she remembers that she and her mother used to sing about the woman warrior when she was yet a child. "After I grew up," Kingston writes, "I heard the chant of Fa Mu Lan, the girl who took her father's place in battle. Instantly, I remembered that as a child I followed my mother about the house, the two of us singing about how Fa Mu Lan fought gloriously and returned alive from war to settle in the village."

Also adding to the confusion surrounding just how much Kingston personally identifies with Fa Mu Lan is Kingston's use of the subjunctive mood—"would"—as the narration transitions from her remembering hearing the talk-story as a child to the actual tale itself, which is told from the first-person "I" perspective of Fa Mu Lan. This narrative technique of using the subjunctive mood begins with Kingston's recalling how her mother told the young Kingston that she would grow up to be a wife and slave, but she rejects these roles and instead promises, "I would have to grow up a warrior woman." This promise is then immediately followed by the transitional section that begins, "The call would come from a bird that flew over our roof," which signals a change in who is narrating the story: "our roof" seems to refer to Kingston and her mother's house, but "The call would come from a bird" begins Fa Mu Lan's story. Only after the old couple on top of the mountain asks Fa Mu Lan if she has eaten yet, and she replies that she already has, does it become clear that the persona of Kingston appears for the last time. After Kingston breaks into the narration at this point and says in a child's pouting voice, "No I haven't. . . . I'm starved. Do you have any cookies? I like chocolate chip cookies," she transitions this modern-day childlike voice into the long-ago voice of Fa Mu Lan, who was seven years old when she began her training as a woman warrior.

The legendary Fa Mu Lan remembers being led by a bird through brambles and over rocks. The narrative then changes to the present tense: Fa Mu Lan finally reaches the summit of a mountain, atop of which stands a thatched hut. There, an old man and an old woman, who represent ultimate wisdom and enlightenment, greet her. They offer to teach her to be a warrior if she will stay with them for fifteen years, but the choice is hers: Either she can return home to pull sweet potatoes in the fields with the rest of her family, or she can become a young woman warrior who will "avenge [her] village" and "recapture the harvests that the thieves have taken." "You can be remembered by the Han people for your dutifulness," the old woman assures her. Fa Mu Lan gladly agrees to stay with the old couple and so spends the next fifteen years undergoing intensive martial arts training in mental and physical activities and disciplines.

The seventh year of Fa Mu Lan's training culminates in a test in which she must demonstrate her survival skills. The old couple leads her—blindfolded—to the mountains of the white tigers, where they abandon her to seek her own way back to their hut, which she eventually finds. Most notable among the many episodes of Fa Mu Lan's ordeal is one in which a white rabbit sacrifices itself for Fa Mu Lan's nourishment. On the brink of despair because she is famished, Fa Mu Lan builds a fire to warm herself and is joined by the white rabbit, which hops close to the woman warrior, sitting next to the fire. Fa Mu Lan resists killing the rabbit, but the animal freely jumps into the flames and turns into meat, "browned just right." "I ate it," Fa Mu Lan explains, "knowing the rabbit had sacrificed itself for me. It made me a gift of meat." This important episode, which symbolizes Fa Mu Lan's attaining enlightenment by refusing selflessly to kill the rabbit, which in turn sacrifices itself for Fa Mu Lan, parallels a similar mythical ordeal attributed to Buddha, the venerated Eastern mystic who preached self-enlightenment. During a period of testing in which the starving Buddha achieved nirvana only after setting aside all thoughts of personal comfort and hunger, a white rabbit immolated itself to feed the hungry man.

For the next eight years, Fa Mu Lan acquires adult wisdom through a training process in "dragon ways." According to traditional Chinese myth, dragons—a metaphor for nature, including the problems and paradoxes in life—encompass the whole world: "The dragon lives in the sky, ocean, marshes, and mountains; and the mountains are also its cranium . . . and sometimes the dragon is one, sometimes many." However, the old couple tells Fa Mu Lan, "You have to infer the whole dragon from the parts you can see and touch." Because dragons are too immense to be seen in their entirety, only by understanding their individual parts can the woman warrior grasp their totality.

Getting to know the different parts of the world as represented by dragons enables Fa Mu Lan to face difficult situations. "I learned to make my mind large," she states, "as the universe is large, so that there is room for paradoxes." In other words, she learns to broaden her mind in order to accept the contradictions in life. And, of course, reconciling cultural paradoxes is what Kingston herself is seeking by writing *The Woman Warrior*: She integrates her mother's talk-stories—and her own versions of these same tales—into her identity as a first-generation Chinese American and, perhaps more significantly, as a *female* Chinese American who is not limited to the subservient gender-biased position that Chinese patriarchal society traditionally demanded of its women.

Throughout her absence from home, Fa Mu Lan views her family and village by looking into a water gourd that the old man possesses. She sees her brother taking their father's place in the army conscription, an act of perfect filial piety—complete obedience and service to one's parents. She also watches her own wedding ceremony, in which her parents wed her to her childhood friend, who marries her despite her absence. He, too, is conscripted into the army.

When the village families are called upon once again to send male family members for service in the army, Fa Mu Lan, having trained for fifteen years with the old couple, returns to her village to take her father's place. Upon arriving, she is showered with glories by her family "as if they were welcoming home a son." However, before her parents allow her to leave to take her father's place in the army, they force her to kneel before the family's ancestral shrine while her father uses a knife to carve a "list of grievances" into her back. Fa Mu Lan does not cry despite the pain. Should she die while fighting in battle, the list, including the oaths, names, and address of her family, will serve to remind everyone of the sacrifices she and her family made.

Fa Mu Lan's father's physically carving words into his daughter's back is a shocking act that seems cruel and inhumane, yet another example of a patriarchal society that sanctions violence against women. Paradoxically, however, his actions are also a testament to the power of language. Fa Mu Lan becomes a text—literally—of written words: "My father first brushed the words in ink, and they fluttered down my back row after row. Then he began cutting; to make fine lines and points he used thin blades, for the stems, large blades." The ideographs, or symbols, of revenge that Fa Mu Lan's father carves into her back transform her into a woman who is revenge incarnate—revenge made flesh. Earlier in the chapter, Kingston noted the bird that led Fa Mu Lan up into the mountains: "In the brush drawings it looks like the ideograph for 'human,' two black wings," and the mountains themselves "look like the ideograph 'mountain.'" By drawing attention to how much these ideographs—revenge, bird, and mountain—look like the very idea or objects that they represent, Kingston emphasizes how language defines experience, which otherwise would remain unrecorded—for example, No Name Woman's life story, or Maxine Hong Kingston's own identity as a female Chinese American.

Her back healed, and now disguised as a man, Fa Mu Lan forms an army of her own rather than fight in anyone else's. Becoming the rallying point for her family, her village, and, eventually, the whole country, she leads her army into battle, fighting for justice and overthrowing the corrupt and morally depraved. Although she remains disguised as a man throughout her crusades, her husband recognizes her, and together they conceive a child. She hides her pregnancy by altering her armor to allow for the increased girth of her waist, and when the child is born, her husband takes him home to his family.

After overthrowing the country's evil emperor and slaying the corrupt baron who had terrorized Fa Mu Lan's village for years, the woman warrior returns to her village to fulfill her filial duties to her husband's family. She declares to his parents, "Now my public duties are finished. . . . I will stay with you, doing farmwork and housework, and giving you more sons." She has also fulfilled her filial duties to her own parents: During her absence, she did not neglect them but rather ensured that her "mother and father and the entire clan would be living happily on the money [she] had sent them." With these words, Fa Mu Lan, the perfect woman warrior, embraces her traditionally female Chinese moral obligations.

Kingston abruptly concludes Fa Mu Lan's story with an ironic proclamation: "My American life has been such a disappointment." Having encouraged us to believe that it is possible for a woman of Chinese descent to gain respect and success, she reveals a sense of betrayal in her mother's talk-stories. She tries to please her mother by modeling herself after Fa Mu Lan, who, she acknowledges, is "the swordswoman who drives me," but when she announces that she earned "straight A's" in school, her mother, instead of praising her daughter, belittles her academic success by reminding her of "a girl who saved her village." Again, as in "No Name Woman," Kingston finds herself confused by the messages in yet another of Brave Orchid's talk-stories. Recalling her sense of confusion, Kingston writes, "I could not figure out what was my village. And it was important that I do something big and fine, or else my parents would sell me when we made our way back to China." To Kingston, who views getting straight A's as something her parents should be proud of, her mother seems to put impossible and confusing demands on her.

What the appropriate role of a village is in relation to its individual members constantly changes throughout the memoir and is one of the major paradoxes that troubles Kingston. Because each female protagonist in *The Woman Warrior* interacts differently with her respective village, Kingston is unable to summarize categorically how a woman should be treated by her village, and what that individual's responsibilities are to her fellow villagers. In "No Name Woman," both Kingston's aunt's family and village ostracize her because she gets pregnant by a man who is not her husband. However, whereas we might then expect No Name Woman to reject her family and certainly her village, her separation from these two social communities is more than she can stand psychologically, and she wavers precipitously between consciousness—represented by comforting thoughts of her family—and unconsciousness—symbolized in her fear of open spaces. Kingston imagines of her aunt, "Flayed, unprotected against space, she felt pain return, focusing her body. . . . For hours she lay on the ground, alternately body and space." No Name Woman's desire to be contained—both physically and socially—within some structure finally drives her to seek refuge in a pigsty: "It was good to have a fence enclosing her, a tribal person alone."

Fa Mu Lan's relationship with her village is diametrically opposite of No Name Woman's with hers. Returning to her home after training for fifteen years with the old couple, Fa Mu Lan is greeted by her parents "as if they were welcoming home a son"; in other words, they are ecstatically happy. The villagers, represented by two cousins of Fa Mu Lan, question where she has been during her absence, but no one takes seriously the possibility that she "went to the city and became a prostitute," as one giggling cousin suggests. When Fa Mu Lan is finally ready to leave her village to fight the evil emperor and tyrannical barons, her departure is radically different from No Name Woman's: The villagers present the woman warrior with gifts—including "their real gifts . . . their sons"—that honor the self-sacrifice that she is making on their behalf. Ironically, the villagers note how beautiful Fa Mu Lan is only *after* she disguises herself as a man; however, they at least acknowledge that this warrior is a *woman* dressed "in man's fashion" when they continue referring to her by using the female pronoun "she": "'How beautiful you look,' the people said. 'How beautiful she looks.'"

Later in the chapter, as Fa Mu Lan and her army approach Peiping, the governmental seat of power, the woman warrior basks in the sight of a united Chinese population acting as one total, all-encompassing community. Although Kingston, of course, created the words she attributes to Fa Mu Lan, even she must realize that her own search for an identity as part of a larger community never will produce the pride and sense of belonging felt by Fa Mu Lan as she looks down at her people from atop a hill: " . . . the land was peopled—the Han people, the People of One Hundred Surnames, marching with one heart, our tatters flying. The depth and width of Joy were exactly known to me: the Chinese population."

Listening to her mother's talk-stories about women warriors, young Kingston does not even understand whether the village that Brave Orchid alludes to when she chides her daughter, "Let me tell you a true story about a girl who saved her village," is the family village in China or the Stockton, California, community in which she and her family live. Because many immigrants considered their stay in America to be temporary, Kingston's parents might have discussed returning with their family to their village in China, which would have confused the young girl trying to fit into an American culture but hearing stories only about China.

Desperate to win her mother's approval and to do something "big and fine," Kingston does not recognize that her mother uses the story of Fa Mu Lan to make the point that sacrificing oneself for the family and village is more important than gaining individual success. Fa Mu Lan's sacrificial acts of fighting in place of her father and saving her village from the tyrannical baron are more important than any actual glory she earns in battle. Brave Orchid downplays her daughter's success at school because, according to the moral of Fa Mu Lan, the self-sacrificial act deserves recognition, not the glory Kingston gets from school, especially since females are not expected to excel in school or in their careers.

As in "No Name Woman," Brave Orchid uses talk-story to provide morals and guidelines for her daughter, who admits of her mother, "At last I saw that I too had been in the presence of great power, my mother talking-story." This admission is especially flattering of Brave Orchid because Kingston uses the same phrase, "the presence of great power," to describe the spirit of the white crane that helped a woman warrior invent white crane boxing. But Kingston interprets Brave Orchid's woman warrior stories differently than her mother intended. Again, because Kingston relates these stories to her personal American context, she reads different meanings into them.

In her own experience as a girl growing up in a Chinese family and community, Kingston knows that girls are not favored. After all, she points out, "There is a Chinese word for the female *I*—which is 'slave.' Break the women with their own tongues!" However, she believes that she could receive the recognition that is reserved for sons if only she traded her female identity for a male's, just as Fa Mu Lan does. Ironically, she finds that by doing things that are considered anti-feminine, she is still unfavored: "I refused to cook. When I had to wash dishes, I would crack one or two. 'Bad girl,' my mother yelled, and sometimes that made me gloat rather than cry. Isn't a bad girl almost a boy?" By giving up her femininity, Kingston also realizes that she will be unsuccessful in getting dates with boys. She finds that the role model provided in the Fa Mu Lan story cannot help her to escape the denigrating remarks made about girls—"Girls are maggots in the rice. It is more profitable to raise geese than daughters"—or to debunk the traditional roles expected of her.

Kingston reveals her disappointment in Fa Mu Lan and shows how the story is of little use to her American reality. For example, when she stands up as a "heroine" to one of her bigoted and chauvinistic American bosses, the real barons in her life, he simply fires her. She also has difficulty understanding why, in Communist China, her aunts and uncles were slaughtered as if *they* were the barons, when in fact they were the villagers who needed saving from the barons' tyrannical rule. She feels tricked by these stories of her descendants because they create paradoxes that she cannot reconcile. One such contradiction involves birds: A bird leads Fa Mu Lan to the old couple on the mountaintop, but birds also lure Kingston's uncle to his death at the hands of the Chinese Communists. Resignedly, Kingston notes, "It is confusing that birds tricked us."

Kingston also cannot conceal her conflicting emotions about wanting to have a family of her own but fearing that to do so would only prove her mother right, that women *are* raised to be only wives and mothers. Jealous of Fa Mu Lan's ability to be swordswoman, wife, and mother, and of the woman warrior's network of support from her family, husband, and village, simultaneously Kingston is angry that she herself does not have any of these things. "Then," she writes, "I get bitter: no one supports me; I am not loved enough to be supported. That I am not a burden has to compensate for the sad envy when I look at women loved enough to be supported." Ironically, the greater she tries to distance herself from her Chinese heritage, the more she realizes just how deeply her mother's talk-stories about her female ancestors have affected her. Although she wants most to identify herself as an individual who lives in America and who has very few ties to China, nevertheless she admits, "Even now China wraps double binds around my feet."

As an adult, Kingston continues to struggle with "dragons," the paradoxes in life. She describes her pain about the emotional distance between herself and her Chinese-born parents in these words: "When I visit the family now, I wrap my American successes around me like a private shawl; I *am* worthy of eating the food. From afar I can believe my family loves me fundamentally. They only say, 'When fishing for treasures in the flood, be careful not to pull in girls,' because that is what one says about daughters." However, there is still a bitter irony in what she says about her parents and her relationship with them.

In the chapter's last paragraph, Kingston finds consolation that she and Fa Mu Lan serve a common purpose. Both women are concerned about the welfare of their people, and both testify to the strength and determination of women who create their own destinies rather than let others decide their futures for them. Fittingly, the Chinese god of war and the Chinese god of literature are one and the same: Kuan Kung. "What we have in common are the words at our backs," Kingston writes, speaking of herself and Fa Mu Lan. "The idioms for *revenge* are 'report a crime' and 'report to five families.' The reporting is the vengeance—not the beheading, not the gutting, but the words. And I have so many words—'chink' words and 'gook' words too—that they do not fit on my skin." Using her gift for talk-story, Kingston fights the many paradoxes in her life with words rather than with a sword.

- **white crane boxing** a style or system of martial arts, or fighting arts.

- **Shao-lin temple** Shaolin, which developed in northern China, is a form of martial arts that emphasizes strength and speed. Martial arts training centers would have been called temples.

- **fighting monks** a Buddhist order of monks trained in martial arts, often depicted in folklore and movies.

- **Confucius** Latinized spelling of the name K'ung-fu-tzu (probably 551–478 B.C.), an itinerant teacher and sage. Three important doctrines of Confucius include believing in benevolence (doing unto others as to yourself), acting with benevolence, and acting in accordance with propriety. Confucius' teachings are recorded in the *Analects*, compiled by his disciples.

- **ideograph** a symbol that represents an idea; for example, the symbol "@" means "at."

- **drinking gourd** a dried and then hollowed-out melon or squash, often oddly shaped, that can be used as a drinking vessel.

- **the Han people** people of the Chinese race; the word "Han" is derived from the name of the dynasty that ruled China from 202 B.C. to A.D. 220.

- **homonyms** words that sound alike but differ in spelling; for example, "meat" and "meet."

- **peony** here, the tree peony, a woody-stemmed perennial with large white or rose-colored flowers that bloom on three- to four-foot stalks. Tree peonies, which grow slowly, are native to western China but have been hybridized in the United States and throughout the world.

- **monk's food** scant, meager portions of food; Fa Mu Lan eats only nuts and dry roots during most of her time on the mountains of the white tigers.

- **fungus** mushrooms.

- **Javanese** pertaining to Java, the most heavily populated of the islands that comprise Indonesia, a country in Southeast Asia.

- **self-immolation** deliberate self-sacrifice, often by burning.

- **transmigration** here, changing physical shape.

- **quarries** excavation pits from which materials such as stones, minerals, or coal are mined.

- **strata** stacked, horizontal layers of rock material.

- **poppies** flowers admired for their beautiful petals; perennial Oriental poppies are best known for their red blossoms with blackish-purple centers.

- **red carp** an inland-water fish common throughout North America, Europe, and Asia; the red carp derives its name from its reddish-colored scales and fins.

- **mallard** a colorful wild duck found throughout North America, Europe, and Asia.

- **cranium** the skull.

- **red money** Giving money is one of the many customs associated with the Chinese New Year, a fifteen-day festival beginning either in late January or early February. The focus of the celebration is the paying of debts, housecleaning, and the ending of quarrels to prepare the way for a peaceful new year. Often the money is given in red envelopes.

- **foreheads tied with wild oaths** scarf-like material wrapped around the forehead and tied at the back of the head; ideographs like those that Fa Mu Lan's father carves on the woman warrior's back would have been stitched into the fabric to spur warriors to perform great deeds.
- **scythes** tools with long, curved blades used for hand-mowing or harvesting grains.
- **descent line** the chronological history of a person's ancestors; a genealogical family tree.
- **baron** socially and economically, the most important group of landowners—next to a country's ruler—during feudal times.
- **conscription** forced drafting into service, usually military.
- **bonded as apprentices** made to serve a specific length of time as a helper to an experienced craftsman; after learning trades through their apprenticeships, apprentices become master craftsmen themselves.
- **Eight Sages** also called the Eight Immortals, eight mythological Chinese men of great wisdom; although unacquainted in real life, the eight are frequently depicted as a group in Chinese art.
- **basin** here, a shallow bowl used to hold water.
- **ink block** a container in which ink is stored.
- **Peiping** means "northern peace"; present-day Beijing, the capital of China.
- **marauders** raiders.
- **fiefdoms** a land-holding system in which large tracts of land are owned and run by feudal lords; mini-kingdoms.
- **Chen Luan-feng** probably a reference to a mythological figure who cut off the leg of Lei Kung, the thunder god, also known as Lei Shen. Lei Kung, who punishes humans guilty of secret crimes, uses a drum and mallet to produce thunder and a chisel to punish wrongdoers.
- **palanquins** Formerly used in eastern Asia, a palanquin is an ornate chair, often covered by a roof to protect the inhabitant and carried on the shoulders of servants using two poles fastened to the chair.
- **sedan chairs** similar to palanquins.
- **gestation** the time period from conception to birth of a baby.
- **paisley** fabric distinguished by its swirling pattern of shapes.

- **nape**   the back of the neck.

- **fontanel**   an anatomical term used to describe a baby's soft membranes between its skull's unformed bones.

- **Long Wall**   the fifteen-hundred-mile Great Wall of China; begun in the third century B.C. as a means of defense against invading marauders from the north.

- **Mongols**   traditionally, the nomadic people of Mongolia, situated north of China; throughout their histories, Mongolia and China always have had a very contentious and uneasy relationship with each other.

- **abacus**   a mathematical device used to solve addition and subtraction problems; invented in China in the twelfth century, the abacus is made up of beads strung on rods in units of ten.

- **the ancestral tablets**   lists on which ancestors' names are inscribed; in ancient China, and to a great extent still today, ancestor worship was universally practiced. Because the dead are believed to have the same needs as the living, the actions of the living affect the dead, and the dead continue to help the living. By tearing down the evil baron's ancestral tablets, Fa Mu Lan defames the evil baron's ancestors and, thus, the evil baron himself.

- **exorcised**   to have cast out evil spirits.

- **Joan of Arc**   (1412–31) the French heroine who, claiming that she regularly talked with dead Catholic saints, inspired the French to victory over the English at Orléans in 1429; she was later captured by the English, tried for heresy, and burned at the stake.

- **CORE**   Congress of Racial Equality; established in 1942 to improve race relations, one of CORE's major projects is voter-registration drives in the South.

- **NAACP**   National Association for the Advancement of Colored People; created in 1909 to help abolish segregation and end discrimination against people of color.

- **Hong Kong**   formerly, a British colony on the southeast coast of Kwangtung Province (Guangdong); Hong Kong reverted to mainland Chinese control in 1997.

- **Fourth Aunt and Uncle**   The title of a relative is accorded by the rank at birth; for example, Third Sister would be the third daughter born into a family.

- **yams**   sweet potatoes, starchy root vegetables often associated with southern U.S. cuisine.
- **faggots**   bundled small branches, frequently used as kindling to start a fire.
- **gurus**   spiritual advisors, or leaders.
- **crank**   here, a person who shams innocent people out of their money.
- **tong ax**   A tong is an association of Chinese individuals in the United States, believed to be involved in organized crime; Kingston speculates that an old busboy whom she encounters is really a swordsman, and that this busboy-swordsman uses an ax to kill people opposed to the tong.
- **flotage**   loose material adrift in water.

"SHAMAN"

Although "No Name Woman" and "White Tigers" are anthologized more often than the other individual chapters in *The Woman Warrior*, "Shaman" is arguably the novel's most pivotal chapter. As the middle chapter in Kingston's memoir about growing up listening to her mother's talk-stories, "Shaman" contains Brave Orchid's personal history: how she earned a medical degree of midwifery in China, then moved to America to be with her husband, and raised their American-born children.

The chapter's title, a tribute to Brave Orchid, refers to a person who acts as a medium between the physical and spiritual worlds, and who usually has healing powers. Brave Orchid is a shaman who exorcises ghosts, both in the Chinese women's school of midwifery and in Stockton, California. In Stockton, for example, when the garbage man walks up to the window from which Kingston and her siblings are taunting him, Brave Orchid hurriedly shuts the window, effectively securing the house from this "Garbage Ghost." However, more important than Brave Orchid's exorcising ghosts is that her story, coming as it does halfway through the novel, provides a transition between events in China and life in America. The novel's first two chapters detail stories based in a Chinese context; the last two chapters focus predominantly on the narrator's and Brave Orchid's lives in America. Bridging the gap between these two opposite realities is the chapter "Shaman," which begins in China but ends in America with Brave Orchid finally accepting that she will never return to China.

Kingston opens this chapter by describing Brave Orchid's three scrolls of medical certificates, a photograph of Brave Orchid herself, and a photograph of the medical school's graduating class. Note that when Kingston opens the canister that contains the scrolls, "the smell of China flies out, . . . a smell that comes from long ago, far back in the brain." Although the phrase "far back in the brain" indicates that the adult Kingston is remembering an event that occurred when she was younger, the phrase also suggests that her impressions of China were somehow subconsciously ingrained in her at birth, as if she could "smell" China because her mother once lived there and smelled odors that she associated with China, and then passed on these sensations to her daughter. However, China remains only a smell to Kingston, an intangibility made all the more confusing by her mother's talk-stories.

Brave Orchid's photographs fascinate Kingston, who notices how differently her mother looks into the camera: "She has spacy eyes, as all people recently from Asia have." Brave Orchid's "spacy" look underscores the intense fear and hesitancy that many Chinese emigrants felt leaving their homeland for America. However, Kingston points out that after these emigrants reside in America for a few years, they "learn the barbarians' directness—how to gather themselves and stare rudely into talking faces as if trying to catch lies." For example, photographs of Kingston's laughing father, who looks directly into the camera and wears a straw hat "cocked at a Fred Astaire angle," show how Westernized he has become since moving to America. Emphasizing the transitional nature of this chapter, Kingston writes that her mother, who has lived in America for many years, now "has eyes as strong as boulders, never once skittering off a face." Also, Brave Orchid's style of dress has dramatically changed. In the medical school class photograph, she wears a dress that suppresses any hint of sexuality: "Chinese dresses at that time were dartless, cut as if women did not have breasts." In old age, Kingston notes toward the chapter's end, Brave Orchid dresses in "American fashions."

Kingston uses the photographs of her mother as a narrative device to introduce Brave Orchid's personal story. Like many Chinese men during the late nineteenth and early twentieth centuries, Brave Orchid's husband—Kingston's father—immigrated to America in search of work. Intending to return to China, instead he sends money to his wife for her boat fare to America. During the time of Brave Orchid's husband's absence, their two Chinese-born children die, and only after a sufficient period of mourning—"In China there was time to complete feelings"—does Brave Orchid decide to attend a medical school of midwifery. Note that on the side of the boat that carries Brave Orchid to the medical school from her hometown, a sea bird is painted to protect the boat against "shipwreck and winds." As in previous chapters, Kingston closely links birds to her family's history; for Brave Orchid, at least, birds bring good luck.

At school, Brave Orchid feels pressure to appear smarter than her fellow classmates: Because she is older than they, traditionally she is expected to be wiser. She seeks out hiding places in which to study secretly so that she will appear more knowledgeable than her peers. These hiding places also symbolize the importance that the female students place on personal space. For example, in her section of the room that she shares with other female students, Brave Orchid "placed precisely" each of her personal items. Her cataloging these items emphasizes the pleasure she gets from organizing her *own* belongings rather than someone else's: "The locks on her suitcase opened with two satisfying clicks; she enjoyed again how neatly her belongings fitted together, clean against the green lining." Although the "daydream of women—to have a room, even a section of a room, that only gets messed up when she messes it up herself"—seems limited at best, most likely the majority of the female students came from homes headed by either a father or a husband, and the women would have been treated by the male figures as second-class citizens in their own homes. "Free from families," Kingston writes, "my mother would live for two years without servitude. She would not have to run errands for my father's tyrant mother with the bound feet or thread needles for old ladies." Ironically, however, "neither would there be slaves and nieces to wait on her."

The incident in which Brave Orchid spends the night in the haunted room and is sat on by a Sitting Ghost recalls many details from the previous two chapters. Kingston begins this section of the narrative with the word "Maybe," which signals that she is reinterpreting her mother's talk-story to understand better how the tale affects her own American life. This narrative strategy is similar to Kingston's inventing a personal history for No Name Woman and introducing Fa Mu Lan's talk-story using the subjective "would." By creating one possible scenario of Brave Orchid's bravery, Kingston emphasizes how her mother is herself a woman warrior, who is unafraid to sleep overnight in a haunted room. Brave Orchid exerts her independent spirit not only when she accepts the other students' challenge to meet whatever ghost awaits her, but intellectually when she daringly questions the traditional belief of life after death: "How do we know that ghosts are the continuance of dead people? . . . Perhaps human beings just die, and that's the end. I don't think I'd mind that too much."

Another, more important example of Brave Orchid's independent, warriorlike spirit is her decision to retain her own name rather than take her husband's after they married. The power to name oneself, to have an individual identity, is further emphasized when Brave Orchid, after arriving in America, keeps her own name rather than Westernize it. "Even when she emigrated," Kingston writes, "my mother kept Brave Orchid, adding no American name nor holding one in reserve for American emergencies." That Brave Orchid retains her own name, that she has a name *at all*, contrasts with Kingston's aunt's namelessness. Kingston suggests throughout the novel that people who control the power of language can survive any ordeal because they cannot lose their personal identities. For example, she notes that when Brave Orchid got scared as a child, "one of my mother's three mothers had held her and chanted their descent line, reeling the frighted spirit back from the farthest deserts." Likewise, after Brave Orchid, who herself is "good at naming," faces the Sitting Ghost at night in the school of midwifery, the following morning the other female students "called out their own names, women's pretty names," to guide Brave Orchid's spirit back to the school. A person like No Name Woman, however, whose identity is figuratively buried along with any memory of her, has no power to stand up for herself and combat the violence inflicted against her. She is a lost soul because her family refuses to call out the list of their ancestors' names in order to guide No Name Woman's spirit back home.

Waiting in the haunted room for the ghost's appearance, Brave Orchid wraps herself in a quilt made by her mother. Of special note is Kingston's description of the quilt: "In the middle of one border my grandmother had sewn a tiny satin triangle, a red heart to protect my mother at the neck, as if she were her baby yet." This protective talisman is identical to the "tiny quilted triangle, red at its center," that Fa Mu Lan had sewn for her baby. The use of the word "quilt" is especially effective in linking Brave Orchid's and Fa Mu Lan's stories. In addition, at the end of "Shaman," Brave Orchid will cover Kingston with a quilt, "the thick, homemade Chinese kind." These images of quilts unite the many woman-warrior influences in Kingston's life.

Two other details recall Fa Mu Lan's story. As Brave Orchid waits for the Sitting Ghost to appear, she reads from a textbook but soon grows tired. Kingston describes the text in Brave Orchid's textbook as her mother's eyes begin to droop: "Soon the ideographs lifted their feet, stretched out their wings, and flew like blackbirds; the dots were their eyes." This description of the textbook's ideographs as birdlike is similar to Kingston's personification of the bird that led Fa Mu Lan to the old couple: "In the brush drawings it looks like the ideograph for 'human,' two black wings." Also, when Brave Orchid first becomes aware of the ghost's presence in the haunted room, Kingston writes of her mother, "She had been pared down like this before, when she had travelled up the mountains into rare snow—alone in white not unlike being alone in black." In "White Tigers," Fa Mu Lan journeyed up into the mountains to gain spiritual enlightenment and became a woman warrior.

After graduating from the women's school of midwifery, Brave Orchid returns as a doctor to her home village, which welcomes her with garlands and cymbals. "My mother wore a silk robe and western shoes with big heels, and she rode home carried in a sedan chair," Kingston writes. "She had gone away ordinary and come back miraculous, like the ancient magicians who came down from the mountains," another reference to Fa Mu Lan. Brave Orchid returns to her village as a medical warrior to save lives. Her reputation grows with every home she visits because she has only success: "She would not touch death; therefore, untainted, she brought only health from house to house."

Although Brave Orchid's intention in telling her personal history to Kingston is to present herself to her daughter as an alternative to the traditional Chinese female roles of child bearer and caretaker, Kingston remains anxious about being a female. Her anxieties stem from listening to her mother's talk-stories about females who are placed in vulnerable positions within Chinese society. One such story involves the village crazy lady, "an inappropriate woman whom the people stoned." Here, Kingston uses the benign adjective "inappropriate" to contrast the woman's insane, uncontrollable actions with the villagers' violent, premeditated killing of her. In the wake of Japanese bombing that "drove people insane," Kingston suggests that the village crazy lady tried to reestablish a personal, ordered identity out of public chaos by wearing a headdress made of mirrors, which attracted the Japanese bombers' attention because the mirrors reflected sunlight and pinpointed where the villagers were hiding. However, the villagers, understandably fearful for their own safety, stone the woman to death rather than simply remove her headdress. For Kingston, this episode must have reminded her of when Brave Orchid warned her in "No Name Woman," "Don't humiliate us . . . The villagers are watchful."

Other sources of Kingston's apprehension about her gender include the stories of baby girls being deliberately suffocated to death in ashes, which account for her recurring nightmares of babies being hurt. Unknowingly, Brave Orchid's sharing these horrific tales with Kingston undercuts any positive effect she might be trying to instill in her daughter. Rather than increase Kingston's self-esteem, these talk-stories cause her to question her own sense of self-worth. "My mother has given me pictures to dream— nightmare babies that recur, shrinking again and again to fit in my palm," Kingston writes. "I curl my fingers to make a cradle for the baby, my other hand an awning. But in a blink of inattention, I would mislay the baby. . . . Or bathing it, I carefully turn the right-hand faucet, but it spouts hot water, scalding the baby until its skin tautens and its face becomes nothing but a red hole of a scream." In this extended passage, note the repetitive "I" that begins each declarative sentence; Kingston tries to reassure herself that she "would protect the dream baby, not let it suffer, not let it out of my sight." However, no matter how many times she dreams of saving the baby, she fails to protect it, and the baby "recedes" from her.

Against this backdrop of dead baby girls and babies who die because they cannot defecate, Kingston struggles to keep her sanity. Her anguish is worsened by her uncertainty as to whether or not her mother might have taken part in these infanticides, or baby killings. "To make my waking life American-normal," she writes, "I turn on the lights before anything untoward makes an appearance. I push the deformed into my dreams, which are in Chinese, the language of impossible stories." Again, China is "invisible," a subconscious world that threatens Kingston most at night. She can *smell* China; she can *hear* China ("my mother funneled China into our ears"); she can even *taste* China ("Mother! Mother! It's happening again. I taste something in my mouth, but I'm not eating anything"); but she cannot *see* China for herself. In contrast, America is the observable, physical world of the every day. Even when Kingston speaks of the innumerable ghosts that surround her in her American life, she differentiates between these intimidating ghosts' physicalness and the unknown—and, therefore, more terrifying—forms of ghosts that she would encounter were she and her family to move to China: "I did not want to go where the ghosts took shapes nothing like our own."

Kingston's childhood fears about the expectations placed on females also stem from Brave Orchid's talk-stories involving female slavery. The sorrowful descriptions of the Chinese girls who are sold as slaves heighten her own fear about being an unwanted daughter who could potentially be sold as a slave were she and her parents to move to China. "Whenever my parents said 'home,'" she writes, "they suspended America. They suspended enjoyment, but I did not want to go to China. In China my parents would sell my sisters and me."

In addition, Kingston struggles with the paradox that Brave Orchid might have favored the quiet girl who was her slave more than Kingston herself: "I watch them with envy," she writes of her mother and the girl. "My mother's enthusiasm for me is duller than for the slave girl." Believing that her mother showed more concern for the slave girl than she does for her own daughters, Kingston suggests that her sister also must compete with this slave for their mother's affection. "Throughout childhood," she explains, "my younger sister said, 'When I grow up, I want to be a slave.'" In "White Tigers," to please her mother, Kingston endeavored to be like Fa Mu Lan, but her attempts to live up to her mother's expectations were ridiculed by Brave Orchid; in "Shaman," her sister chooses the girl-slave as a model. However, Kingston's sister's wanting to win her mother's affection by taking on this role is paradoxical: She will have to accept that she is an unwanted daughter since only unwanted daughters are sold or given away as slaves.

Kingston also finds it contradictory that her mother, who is medically trained as a midwife, could believe in superstitions. As an adult writing the stories of her mother's encounters with ghosts and monsters, she must recognize the deep vein of ingrained Chinese lore in Brave Orchid's talk-stories. She suspects that all of the women at the To Keung School of Midwifery were like her mother's three female roommates, who eagerly obeyed Brave Orchid and pulled earlobes and chanted spirits away. Although Kingston writes that the students were "new women, scientists who changed the rituals," despite their scientific training they continued to believe in ghosts and other spirits, a contradiction that the adult Kingston cannot reconcile.

However, as a child, the impressionable Kingston believes in her mother's extraordinary exorcistic abilities. Left on her own to make sense of her mother's stories, Kingston recalls one perplexing story in which Brave Orchid confronts "Sit Dom Kuei," ghosts that appear as snake-like whirlwinds. Because of her limited understanding of the Chinese language, Kingston cannot translate what "Sit Dom Kuei" means, except that "Kuei" is Chinese for ghost. Hopelessly asking "How do they translate?" Kingston's language fails her, ironically because Chinese is not her native language. Also, her inability to translate "Sit Dom Kuei" is another symbol of the cultural gap that separates her from her parents. Only at the memoir's end, after having secured a private, personal identity as an adult, a woman, a Chinese American, an American, will Kingston confidently proclaim about her own talk-story, "It translated well."

In "Shaman," as in the previous chapters, Kingston cannot ask Brave Orchid questions and expect understandable answers that are relevant to her own life. Instead, she depends on her own imagination and concludes only that her mother, like the legendary figures about whom she talk-stories, was powerful against ghosts because she could eat anything and everything. In making this conclusion, Kingston begins to accept that she will need to reconcile, or learn to live with, the differences between her American life and the values and practices expected of her in her Chinese home life. However, integrating her mother's horrific talk-stories into her American life, or at least discounting their believability to lessen their vivid sensationalism, severely threatens Kingston's psychological stability. For example, when she endures yet another telling of the monkey story, in which participants sit around a table and literally eat the brain of a monkey, whose head is trapped within a cutout hole in the table's middle, Kingston unsettlingly writes, "a curtain flapped loose inside my brain." She is so horrendously shocked by this gruesome account that she again loses the power of language and is unable to tell her mother, "Stop it." This account's graphic depiction is intensified even more when we—and Kingston—learn that the monkey was *alive* when the participants began eating its brain. "It was alive?" Kingston incredulously asks. "The curtain flaps closed like merciful black wings." In addition, Kingston directly follows this talk-story with her mother's telling her children, "Eat! Eat!" Humorously, what Brave Orchid wants them to eat—"blood pudding awobble in the middle of the table"—looks too akin to the monkey brain that they have just heard about to be inviting.

In the last section of "Shaman," which chronologically takes place after the next two chapters, Brave Orchid confronts Kingston about why she doesn't visit her parents more than once a year. "The last time I saw you," Brave Orchid exaggeratedly complains, "you were still young." Although both women still hold decidedly opposite outlooks on life, Kingston emphasizes that she and her mother are not as different as she perhaps would like to believe. Physically, both women have white hair; emotionally, they are equals who have strong, independent identities. However, Kingston is painfully aware that her mother is slowly losing her will to live, to function independently of her husband and children. At one point in this section, Kingston chides her mother not to eat pills lying around the house if they are not hers: "You shouldn't take pills that aren't prescribed for you. 'Don't eat pills you find on the curb,' you always told us." Like many adults with parents who are aging quickly, Kingston is becoming the caregiver to her mother, who previously was the caregiver to Kingston.

Brave Orchid's complaint that she does not see Kingston often enough introduces a preoccupation with time that dominates Kingston and Brave Orchid's conversation here at the end of the chapter. Earlier, Kingston noted that even after her mother began living in America, Brave Orchid never stopped "seeing land on the other side of the oceans." Brave Orchid's goal was to return someday to her Chinese ancestral village and live out her life there, but now she admits that she and Kingston's father will never return to their homeland. "We have no more China to go home to," she concedes. This realization is apparent in the answer she gives when Kingston asks her about the two children who died in China: "No, you must have been dreaming. You must have been making up stories. You are all the children there are." Whether or not Brave Orchid truly has suppressed memories of her life in China now that she knows that she can never return to the land of her birth is unclear. The possibility remains that her memories of her two dead children are too painful to discuss, much like No Name Woman's family refused to honor her memory.

Culturally, Brave Orchid and Kingston perceive time differently. Brave Orchid honestly believes that time in China is paced more slowly than in America: "Human beings don't work like this in China. Time goes slower there. . . . I can't sleep in this country because it doesn't shut down for the night." For her, China symbolizes youth because that is where she spent the earlier years of her life. "Time was different in China," she reasons. "One year lasted as long as my total time here. . . . I would still be young if we lived in China." For Kingston, however, "time is the same from place to place." Time is universal because geographical location is universal: We all share the same earth, no matter where on it we are physically located.

Kingston exhibits concern and caring as Brave Orchid's caregiver by helping her mother understand that China is still as much a part of Brave Orchid's world as America is. Hoping to arouse her mother's defeated spirit, Kingston tries to reason with her: "We belong to the planet now, Mama. Does it make sense to you that if we're no longer attached to one piece of land, we belong to the planet? Wherever we happen to be standing, why, that spot belongs to us as much as any other spot." Struggling to comprehend her daughter's meaning, Brave Orchid seems to have forgotten that earlier in the chapter, while she was waiting for the Sitting Ghost to appear, she herself voiced a similar thought in relation to the moon and stars: "'That is the same moon that they see in New Society Village,' she thought, 'the same stars.'" And, in the parenthetical sentence directly following Brave Orchid's thought, Kingston notes that growing up, she heard her mother similarly say, "That is the same moon that they see in China, the same stars though shifted a little."

Although Brave Orchid remains inconsolable at the chapter's end, both she and Kingston gain a better understanding of one another from their conversation. Brave Orchid genuinely accepts that her daughter visits her only once a year because physically and emotionally she needs that separation from her parents to keep her sanity. When Kingston tells her mother, "Here I'm sick so often, I can barely work. I can't help it, Mama," Brave Orchid finally acknowledges her daughter's needs: "It's better, then, for you to stay away. . . . Of course, you must go, Little Dog." The affectionate term "Little Dog," perhaps prompted by Kingston's own use of the childlike "Mama," greatly affects Kingston, who now understands that her mother loves her even if she doesn't say that she does. "The world is somehow lighter," Kingston contentedly writes. "She has not called me that endearment for years—a name to fool the gods."

The dragon imagery at the end of the chapter symbolizes a resolution between Brave Orchid and Kingston. Earlier, when Brave Orchid faced the Sitting Ghost, Kingston wrote, "My mother may have been afraid, but she would be a dragoness ('my totem, your totem')." Here at the chapter's close, Kingston reaffirms that she and Brave Orchid are both women warriors: "I am really a Dragon, as she is a Dragon, both of us born in dragon years. I am practically a first daughter of a first daughter." Although the chapter's last paragraph strongly suggests that nights still hold unseen terrors for Kingston, she tacitly acknowledges that she owes her creative abilities to Brave Orchid, whose talk-stories are the impetus for Kingston's own power of language as a woman warrior, as a dragon in her own right.

- **Canton** known today as Guangzhou, the largest city in south China and the capital of Kwangtung Province (Guangdong); it is one of China's main commercial centers.

- **Singapore** an island country in Southeast Asia controlled by the British from 1824 to 1965; the city of Singapore is the country's capital.

- **Taiwan** an island country less than a hundred miles southeast of mainland China; in 1949, Chinese Communist forces drove Chiang Kai-shek, the leader of the Kuomintang, which means "national people's party," and other Chinese Nationalists to this island, formerly known as Formosa, where they established the Republic of China—in contrast to the *People's Republic of China*, which is Communist mainland China.

- **midwifery** the practice of a midwife, a person—usually a woman—who assists women during childbirth.

- **pediatrics** the medical field that specializes in the care of infants and children.

The Woman Warrior

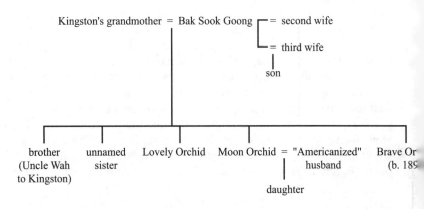

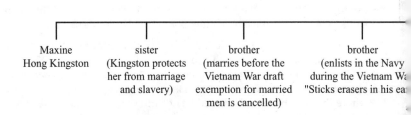

China Men Genealogy

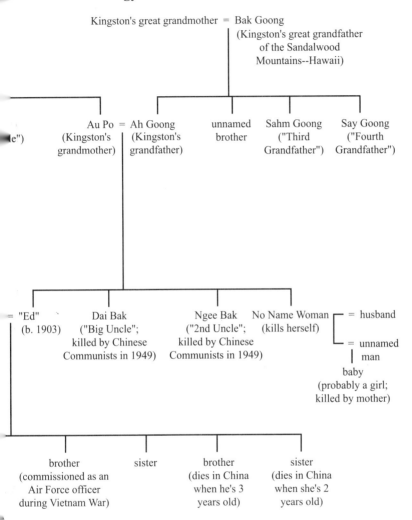

- **gynecology** the medical field devoted to the healthcare of women and their reproductive organs.
- **"Medecine"** medicine.
- **"Surgary"** surgery.
- **therapeutics** the treatment of diseases, either by medical science or holistic means.
- **ophthalmology** the medical field that specializes in the care of eyes.
- **bacteriology** the study of bacteria.
- **dermatology** the study of skin.
- **embossed** carved or adorned.
- **"Ex-assistant étranger à la clinique chirugicale et d'accouchement de l'université de Lyon"** French, meaning "The former foreign assistant at the surgical and birthing clinic of the University of Lyon [France]."
- **zinnia** a stiff, hairy-stemmed flower with a single flower head; except for blue, zinnias bloom in all colors.
- **chrysanthemum** also called mums; a popular garden plant that has large flower heads.
- **Coney Island** during the 1920s, a popular amusement park and famous boardwalk located in Brooklyn, New York, along the Atlantic Ocean waterfront.
- **biplane** an airplane with two sets of wings, one set over the engine and the other located on the tail; during World War I, and through the early 1930s, biplanes dominated both military and commercial aviation.
- **Fred Astaire** (1899–1987) Hollywood's famous male dancer who teamed with Ginger Rogers in ten popular movies for RKO Studio during the 1930s, including *Top Hat* (1935) and *Swing Time* (1936).
- **concierge** generally, a hotel employee who assists guests; Brave Orchid is fortunate that the To Keung School of Midwifery provides a concierge for its students.
- **largess** generosity.
- **figs** the fruit of the fig tree, a Mediterranean tree or shrub; gathered when they fall from the tree and then dried, figs are so widely used in Mediterranean countries that they are called "the poor man's food."
- ***yang* and *yin*** *Yang* is the masculine element of Chinese philosophy—that is, aggressive, hot, active, dry, and bright qualities. *Yin* is the femi-

nine element of Chinese philosophy—that is, receptive, cool, inactive, moist, and dark qualities.

- **Sun Yat-sen**   (1866–1925) leader of the Chinese Kuomintang, a political party that overthrew the Manchu dynasty in 1911; Sun served as the first provisional president of the Republic of China (1911–12) and later as its de facto ruler (1923–25).
- **gnomes**   mythological dwarflike creatures who live underground.
- **adamantine chin**   a strong-looking chin.
- **totem**   an object or animal used to represent membership in a group, clan, or family.
- **talismans**   objects that supposedly give their owners magical powers; for example, a rabbit's foot is a popular good-luck talisman.
- **ferule**   a rod used to punish children.
- **Kwangtung Province**   also called Guangdong, a province of southeast China; incorporated into China in 222 B.C., when the first emperor of the Ch'in dynasty conquered the area.
- **Gobi Desert**   a desert that extends from southeast Mongolia south into northern China.
- **whorls**   spiraling forms; for example, a tornado.
- **surfeited**   excessive.
- **tarry oil**   thick, black oil made from tar.
- **boas**   large snakes that coil around and suffocate their prey; or, long scarves made of soft material, such as feathers or fur, wrapped around the neck or slung over the shoulder.
- **lion**   here, a large puppet, like a parade float, but manually operated, probably by men inside the lion.
- **lichees**   the nutlike fruit of the litchi, or lichee tree, indigenous to China.
- **zenith**   here, the highest region of the sky.
- **nadir**   the diametrical opposite of the zenith; an astronomical term representing the lowest point below the observer.
- **phoenix notes**   Traditionally, only one phoenix, a fictional bird from ancient eastern Mediterranean lore, lives at any given time. The one-of-a-kind phoenix lives its five-hundred-year life span, then climbs onto a funeral pyre, and sets itself aflame. From its ashes springs a worm that

develops into a new phoenix decked in radiant red, purple, and gold plumage. The Chinese believe that the song of the phoenix is especially beautiful, and that the phoenix has an appreciation for human music.

- **metempsychosis** reincarnation, the belief that after the human body dies, its soul is reborn—in human, animal, or even vegetable form; this process continues until the soul reaches perfection. Buddhists believe that the soul has five skandhas, or groups of elements: body, sensations, perceptions, impulses, and consciousness. In death, the soul ceases to exist, but its karma—perhaps what Kingston alludes to as the six paths, the five skandhas plus karma—is reborn in a mother's womb, in the body of a new baby. This system of regeneration continues until a person reaches the state of nirvana, in which personal desires do not exist.

- **Ch'in** the Ch'in dynasty (221–206 B.C.), from which China gets its name.

- **hexagrams that are the *I Ching*** The *I Ching*, or "Book of Changes," the majority of which was written by Wen Wang (twelfth century B.C.), is an ancient Chinese text concerning Confucianism. Of great importance in the history of Chinese philosophy, the work explains ethical principles through a system that involves the oneness of humans and nature in daily communion. The complex hexagrams—six-sided figures—of the *I Ching* represent different positive qualities; the more hexagrams you "build" on top of one another, the closer you are to an understanding of the world.

- **anemia** a deficiency of red blood cells, which contain hemoglobin, an oxygen-carrying pigment; because one symptom of anemia is paleness of tissue and the skin, Brave Orchid checks the color of the tissue under the female slave's eyelids.

- **felicitous** pleasing.

- **pantomimed** here, communicated using hand gestures.

- **were-people** for Kingston, another term meaning ghosts, or spirits.

- **cervixes** necks, or other necklike structures.

- **nether** underground, or the underworld.

- **Animalcules** microscopic organisms.

- **Chung-li Ch'uan** one of the Eight Sages who probably lived sometime between 206 B.C. and A.D. 220; he is usually depicted as a fat, bearded, wine-drinking hermit.

- **night soil buckets** portable containers used primarily for nighttime urine.

- **magpies**   Related to jays, magpies have long tails, black-green plumage, and white markings over their shoulders.
- **sea swallow**   also known as terns, graceful water birds that inhabit seacoasts and inland waters; most terns, which form breeding colonies of millions of individuals, lay their eggs on the ground, and in some parts of the world, including Malaya, their eggs are gathered for human consumption.
- **Malaya**   the peninsula directly south of Thailand, in Southeast Asia; Malaya gained its independence from British rule in 1957, and became part of the Federation of Malaysia in 1963.
- **hairpin**   a small metal clip used to hold hair in place.
- **magistrate**   a government employee who administers and enforces the law.
- **Shantung**   means "Eastern Mountains"; a northern coastal province in China, including the Shantung Peninsula, and China's third most populous province.
- **Changchow**   also known as Changzhou, a city in eastern China, west of Shanghai.
- **yellow croaker**   a saltwater fish; in China, yellow croakers are caught mainly in Kwangtung Province, which supplies about one-fifth of the fish consumed in China.
- **Hanchow**   possibly Hangchow, a city southwest of Shanghai, in Chekiang Province; capital city of the Southern Sung dynasty (960–1279).
- **ingots**   any standardized shapes of metal; for example, gold bars.
- **bantams**   small, aggressive chickens.
- **purple dromedaries**   one-humped camels; "purple" dromedaries are only imaginary.
- **First Emperor of Ch'in**   refers to Chao Cheng, who came to the throne in 247 B.C., and, by 221 B.C., had solidified the Ch'in dynasty, mostly through conquests of rival territories; during the Ch'in empire, which lasted until 206 B.C., the Great Wall of China was begun, and all books except those on such subjects as medicine were burned to halt subversive thought.
- **jasper**   a red, yellow, or brown variety of the mineral quartz.
- **Mount Fuji**   Japan's highest mountain, located sixty miles southwest of Tokyo; Mount Fuji, which is sacred to the Japanese, is a volcano, dormant since 1707 but still classified as "active" by geologists.

- **strafed** randomly attacked with machine-gun or cannon fire.
- **Li T'ieh-kuai** one of the Eight Immortals; Li is depicted as an old man, with a gourd slung over his shoulder; the gourd holds medicine, which Li dispenses to the poor, and at night serves as his bedroom.
- **impish** mischievous.
- **Ellis Island** an island off of New York City that served as the primary immigration station from 1892 to 1943.
- **dirigibles** airships, or blimps.
- **atavistic** the reappearance of some characteristic in a family bloodline that has not been evident for generations.
- **rheumatism** inflammation of muscles or joints, causing stiffness and pain.
- **varicose veins** blood-swollen veins, commonly occurring in the legs.
- **tubercular handkerchiefs** Tuberculosis is an infectious disease caused by bacteria, called tubercle bacillus; because the disease can be spread from person to person, people already infected with tuberculosis would hold handkerchiefs or other material to their mouths whenever they coughed to lessen the chance of spreading the disease.
- **lepers' socks** Leprosy is a chronic disease characterized by skin sores, gangrene, and even paralysis; because the disease is contagious, people with leprosy—known as lepers—often cover their skin to restrain the disease from spreading and because of the social stigma attached to the disease.
- **peat dirt** highly organic soil derived from peat, decomposed vegetable matter used as a fertilizer and, in some countries, as a fuel.
- **chick mash** highly nutritious food fed to baby chicks.
- **loquat tree** a small evergreen tree, native to China and Japan, with white flowers and yellow, edible fruit.
- **Romany** Romany is a catchall word that means gypsy, the language that gypsies speak, and the location from which gypsies come, although Romany is not a physical country or place.

"AT THE WESTERN PALACE"

Kingston, who in "Shaman" narrated the personal talk-story of her mother, Brave Orchid, now relates the failed assimilation into American culture of Brave Orchid's younger sister, Moon Orchid, whose inability to adapt to a new, American way of life destines her first to insanity and then to death. Estranged from her husband for thirty years after he left China and moved to America, Moon Orchid arrives in America from Hong Kong, where she lived a very comfortable life thanks to her husband, who regularly sent money to support her and their daughter, but who never personally corresponded with his Chinese family. He does not know that Brave Orchid has arranged for her sister to immigrate to America.

Unlike the other chapters in *The Woman Warrior*, "At the Western Palace" is narrated by a third-person narrator, who relates the talk-story about Kingston's aunt by constructing a linear plot progression. The chapter opens at the San Francisco airport, where sixty-eight-year-old Brave Orchid has been waiting for over nine hours for Moon Orchid's arrival. She is irritated that her children are wandering around the airport rather than sitting quietly with her. Moon Orchid's daughter, whom Brave Orchid also helped emigrate from China, and who has not seen her mother for five years, sits patiently with her aunt. Brave Orchid has been awake since before her sister's airplane took off from Hong Kong, intent on adding her "will power to the forces that keep an airplane up." When she sees a group of soldiers and sailors in the airport terminal, she suddenly remembers that her own son is serving in the Vietnam War. Forced now to split her shamanic powers between her sister's safety and her son's safety, her head hurts from the concentration in keeping Moon Orchid's plane airborne and her son's ship afloat. Anxious about this son, whom she considers to be a heedless boy who will surely die in the war, she divulges her worries about him to her niece. Her other children can take care of themselves, she says, but this son is not normal: He "sticks erasers in his ears, and the erasers are still attached to the pencil stubs. The captain will say, 'Abandon Ship,' or, 'Watch out for bombs,' and he won't hear."

In this episode, in which Brave Orchid waits for Moon Orchid to arrive from Hong Kong, Brave Orchid contrasts her children's behavior with her niece's. She is highly critical of her children's impatience, which she characterizes as a distinctly *American* trait; however, her niece's sitting with her impresses Brave Orchid as proper, respectful, *Chinese* deportment. "Her American children could not sit for very long," Brave Orchid muses to herself. "They did not understand sitting; they had wandering feet." She thinks of them as a "bad boy and bad girl," but her niece's opinion of her cousins is very different. For example, when Brave Orchid complains that her son in Vietnam is careless and "not normal," her niece defends him and his siblings. Speaking to her aunt, she says, "Your son can take care of himself. All your children can take care of themselves."

Brave Orchid does not understand that her children, in addition to caring for themselves, also protect her from situations that would upset her. Such is the case when Brave Orchid accuses her children of hiding letters written to her by her son in Vietnam. Because they know that Brave Orchid wanted her son to flee to Canada to avoid being drafted, and that she worries about his safety, they hide his letters to shield her from the constant threat of his being killed in war.

When Moon Orchid finally arrives at the airport, Brave Orchid is shocked by how old her sister looks. Earlier, Brave Orchid mistakenly identified a young woman as Moon Orchid, but her niece cautiously explained that Moon Orchid would look much older than the woman whom Brave Orchid believed to be her sister. Brave Orchid's initially identifying this young woman as Moon Orchid recalls the conversation between herself and Kingston at the end of "Shaman," in which Brave Orchid contended that time in China moves more slowly than in America, and that had she remained in China, she would be young still. Remembering that this previous conversation between Brave Orchid and Kingston chronologically occurs *after* the events in "At the Western Palace," Brave Orchid's continuing to believe in "Shaman" that time is somehow suspended in China, even after she sees how old her newly arrived, younger sister is, emphasizes how strongly ingrained are her misperceptions of her former homeland, and how wholly she identifies herself as Chinese, not Chinese American. Even during the car ride to Stockton, Brave Orchid and Moon Orchid keep saying "Aiaa! How old!" whenever they look disbelievingly at one another.

Back at home, Brave Orchid wants to perform a luck ceremony to welcome her sister, but Moon Orchid tells everyone to open the presents that she has brought for them. She becomes totally immersed in giving out the gifts, including a paper doll of Fa Mu Lan, who, Moon Orchid assures her nieces and nephews, "really existed." Brave Orchid considers these presents frivolous and extravagant.

Unlike Moon Orchid, she is particularly wary of extravagances that may draw the attentions of jealous gods. Eventually, Brave Orchid has her luck ceremony, feeding candy to her children: "It was very important that the beginning be sweet." The sisters then prepare a huge dinner for the family.

Brave Orchid and her children's personal interactions during Moon Orchid's gift-giving are strained at best. The cultural gap between them is immense, in large part because Brave Orchid judges her children based on traditional Chinese manners. For example, when Moon Orchid passes out the paper dolls, the children immediately begin to play with them. However, Brave Orchid, raised by Chinese parents who taught her "correct" Chinese behavior, privately thinks of her children, "How greedy to play with presents, in front of the giver." This relationship between tradition and behavior is addressed most directly when Brave Orchid remembers that the Chinese word for "impolite" is "untraditonal." She characterizes her children as lazy, and when they balk at eating the luck-ceremony candy that symbolizes good beginnings, she thinks of them as stupid: "They'd put the bad mouth on their aunt's first American day; you had to sweeten their noisy barbarous mouths."

Another reason for the breakdown of Brave Orchid and her children's relationship is their lack of meaningful communication. Kingston recalls that when she was growing up, on certain occasions her mother opened the front door and mumbled something, and then opened the back door and mumbled again. Whenever the children asked her what and why she mumbled, Brave Orchid refused to interpret her actions. "It's nothing," she would say to her children. "She never explained anything that was really important. They no longer asked." In addition, at the supper table, Brave Orchid always invoked silence and did not allow anyone to speak—at least, not in Chinese. Kingston notes that children in other families whose parents forbade talking at the supper table created an elaborate sign language to overcome their parents' enforced silence. She and her siblings, however, talked freely in English, "which their parents didn't seem to hear." Because Brave Orchid does not consider English to be a "language," the children may speak it without getting into trouble. Unfortunately, this language barrier dramatically increases the cultural gap between Brave Orchid and her children: Brave Orchid will not master English because it symbolizes the barbarous American culture, and the children resist speaking Chinese because they want to be "American-normal."

Although Brave Orchid regularly denigrates American culture, which she views as wasteful and uncivilized, she is not immune to its effects. One example of her relaxing the many Chinese customs with which she was raised is the American practice of hanging pictures of living relatives on walls in the house, in this case her and her husband's own portraits. When Moon Orchid notices that her sister's and brother-in-law's pictures hang opposite her grandparents' and asks why, Brave Orchid casually remarks, "No reason. Nothing. . . . In America you can put up anybody's picture you like." Her answer appears to be insignificant at first, but its import is great: No matter how much she resists the American culture around her, it affects her more than she might be willing to admit. Also, she hangs the pictures because "later the children would not have the sense to do it."

After dinner, although it is late at night and Moon Orchid is tired from her long journey, Brave Orchid insists that Moon Orchid and Moon Orchid's daughter "get down to [the] business" of reuniting Moon Orchid with her husband. She wants to talk about the glorious moment in which her sister will confront her brother-in-law and reclaim her marriage rights: "Oh, how I'd love to be in your place. I could tell him so many things. What scenes I could make." For the last thirty years, Moon Orchid has been receiving money from her husband, but she has never told him that Brave Orchid had been planning to bring her to America: "She waited for him to suggest it, but he never did." She is frightened at the prospect of confronting her husband, but Brave Orchid is adamant that her sister should reclaim her rightful place as "Big Wife"—the first-married wife of a husband. Although Brave Orchid knows that the husband has a second wife, whom he married after he arrived in America, she does not consider this "Little Wife" a barrier to her sister and brother-in-law's reconciliation: Customarily, a wealthy Chinese man in China was married simultaneously to more than one woman.

Moon Orchid and her daughter stay with Brave Orchid for several weeks, a difficult time for Brave Orchid and her children. Brave Orchid is impatient with her sister, whom she regards as the "lovely, useless type." Moon Orchid is unable to do manual work either in the house or in the family-owned laundry. Because the laundry is unbearably hot, the most she can learn to do is fold towels late in the day, when the temperature inside the laundry has cooled. Used to a life of comfort, she is "eager to work, roughing it in the wilderness," but anything she attempts to do infuriates Brave Orchid because she works too slowly.

Moon Orchid's stay with Brave Orchid reveals how very different these two sisters are. Brave Orchid represents frugality and tradition; Moon Orchid is frivolous, extravagant, and ephemeral. Their contrasting identities are best embodied in their names: Brave Orchid is "brave"; Moon Orchid, whose name means "flower of the moon," is like a planet circling the sun, a body in orbit around her distant husband. Brave Orchid believes that a wife's primary role is to "scold her husband into becoming a good man"; her sister passively accepts whatever her husband tells her to do, even if that means not being a part of his America life.

Brave Orchid has a strong, overpowering personality that assertively exerts itself in any situation. Single-mindedly determined that Moon Orchid should confront her "barbarian" husband, Brave Orchid exudes unquestioned confidence that any one of the many possible scenarios she devises for Moon Orchid to accost her husband will succeed. Brave Orchid is so totally consumed by her sister's plight that she fails to realize that Moon Orchid's passive, non-confrontational demeanor will not allow her to confront her husband. Note how often Brave Orchid discusses how *she* would act if *she* were in her sister's stead. For example, strategizing how best Moon Orchid can impress her husband, Brave Orchid says, "Another thing I'd do if I were you, I'd get a job and help him out. Show him I could make his life easier; how I didn't need his money." However, Brave Orchid is not her sister: She relishes the dramatic opportunity to face her brother-in-law; Moon Orchid would rather move back to Hong Kong.

In contrast to Brave Orchid, Moon Orchid emerges as delicate and vacillating, happiest when following the lead of others. Physically, she has "long fingers and thin, soft hands." Her "high-class city accent from living in Hong Kong" symbolically reveals a frail woman who has never worked in her life, and who has had servants fulfill her every need. Brave Orchid contemptuously remarks of her "wishy-washy" sister, "Not a trace of village accent remained; she had been away from the village for that long." Brave Orchid also notes that "bright colors and movements distracted her" like they would a child. Faced with the looming threat of confronting her unsuspecting husband, Moon Orchid would choose—were it not for her sister's constant nagging—to remain estranged from him. "Do we have to do something?" she passively asks.

Moon Orchid's stay with Brave Orchid and her family also exposes the ever-present cultural gap between Brave Orchid and her children. This rift is caused, in part, by Brave Orchid's failure to realize that many traditional Chinese customs are not adaptable to American culture. For example, when Brave Orchid tries to convince Moon Orchid that her estranged husband's children by his second wife will recognize Moon Orchid as their mother, she tells her sister, "The children will go to their true mother—you. . . . That's the way it is with mothers and children." But that is *not* the way it is with Brave Orchid and her own children, who, Brave Orchid admits, are "antisocial and secretive." "Ever since they were born," she recalls, "they had burrowed little nests for themselves in closets and underneath stairs; they made tents under tables and behind doors." Because the children live in a home so totally dominated by their autocratic mother, who rejects their assimilation into American culture, they physically construct hiding places to escape emotionally from her control and to create individualized, "American-normal" identities.

Brave Orchid's children find Moon Orchid's behavior odd, as she does theirs. The running commentary that Moon Orchid provides as she follows them about the house emphasizes just how Americanized Kingston and her siblings are. Growing up, Moon Orchid was taught to look demurely askance at adults, never directly into their eyes; her sister's children, however, look straight into her eyes, "as if they were looking for lies. . . . They were like animals the way they stared." Traditionally, Chinese custom considered a person polite who denied, not accepted, a compliment, but Moon Orchid's nieces and nephews receive her compliments unashamedly. Initially, Moon Orchid suspects that Brave Orchid's children are "animals" who live in a barbarian culture; her suspicion is confirmed when she sees them eat undercooked meat. Worse, they are "savages" who always smell like cow's milk: "At first she thought they were so clumsy, they spilled it on their clothes. But soon she decided they themselves smelled of milk. They were big and smelled of milk; they were young and had white hair." Moon Orchid does not realize that many Americans drink milk their entire lives, but neither do Brave Orchid's children know that in traditional Chinese society, only babies drink milk.

When Moon Orchid's daughter must return to Los Angeles to her own family, Brave Orchid decides that it is also time for Moon Orchid to rejoin her husband. She forces her unwilling son to drive them all to Los Angeles. During the journey, Brave Orchid continues to imagine the approaches that Moon Orchid should take in confronting her husband and reclaiming her rights as his wife. Moon Orchid, however, remains unsure of herself, especially now that she has read in a newspaper that it is unlawful for an American man to be married to more than one woman at a time. "The law doesn't matter," Brave Orchid says to bolster her sister's confidence.

On the way to Los Angeles, Brave Orchid narrates a talk-story about an emperor with four wives, from which this chapter gets its ironic title. "A long time ago," Brave Orchid begins, an emperor had four wives, each of whom lived in a palace located at one of the earth's four major compass points. The Empress of the East, whom Brave Orchid likens to Moon Orchid, was "good and kind and full of light," but the Empress of the West, in her striving for ultimate power over the emperor's other three wives, imprisoned the emperor in the Western Palace. Only Moon Orchid, the Empress of the East, can save the emperor, her husband, from the evil clutches of the Empress of the West, her husband's second wife with whom he is living. "You must break the strong spell she has cast on him that has lost him the East," Brave Orchid encourages her sister.

Although Brave Orchid's talk-story about the emperor and his four wives is the shortest talk-story—only one paragraph—in *The Woman Warrior*, it is the best example of how talk-stories are meant to empower individuals. To Brave Orchid, the talk-story justifies her and her sister's moral righteousness in confronting the barbarian husband and his barbarian wife, and guarantees success for their mission. Knowing that Moon Orchid lacks the courage needed to confront her husband and demand the respect from him that she deserves, Brave Orchid attempts to bolster her sister's resiliency, to strengthen her mentally by likening her to a woman warrior who comes out of the dawn to "free the Emperor." Stylistically, note the magical, mystical images that Kingston uses to introduce this otherworldly, mythological realm of emperors and empresses: "They set out at gray dawn, driving between the grape trees, which hunched like dwarfs in the fields. Gnomes in serrated outfits that blew in the morning wind came out of the earth, came up in rows and columns. Everybody was only half awake." In only three sentences, we are transported into a wholly different world, a new reality in which women warriors fight for what they believe is right and just.

At times during the trip to Los Angeles, Moon Orchid grows momentarily confident in her ability to confront her husband, but as she approaches Los Angeles, she becomes more terrified than ever. However, Brave Orchid orders her son to continue the journey, and they track Moon Orchid's husband's address to a downtown skyscraper. There, Brave Orchid makes a reconnaissance visit to determine how best to surprise Moon Orchid's husband. She discovers that he is a brain surgeon, and that his Chinese-American wife, whom Brave Orchid describes as a "modern, heartless girl," works with him as a nurse. She also notes how poorly this second wife speaks Chinese. To get the husband alone, Brave Orchid devises a plan to trick him into leaving his office so that he can meet the sisters in their car on the street.

When the husband arrives at the car, Brave Orchid and Moon Orchid are taken aback by how commanding, young, and American he looks: "The two old ladies saw a man, authoritative in his dark Western suit, start to fill the front of the car. He had black hair and no wrinkles. He looked and smelled like an American." Initially, he unknowingly addresses Moon Orchid and her sister as "Grandmothers," but when he finally recognizes who they are, he is angry at Moon Orchid. Demanding to know why she has come to Los Angeles and what she wants, he tells her that she is mistaken if she thinks that she can fit into his new American life. Although he does not want her to return to China ("I wouldn't wish that on anyone"), he also does not want her to visit him again. His second wife does not know that he has a Chinese family, and in America he could be arrested for having two wives. While he is prepared to continue supporting Moon Orchid financially, he will not acknowledge her in his home.

This episode, in which Moon Orchid unsuccessfully confronts her husband, emphasizes how important language is to personal identity. As Moon Orchid sits in the car outside her husband's office building, her confidence wanes in direct relation to her losing her ability to talk: "I won't be able to talk," she tells her sister. "And sure enough, her voice was fading into a whisper. She was shivering and small in the corner of the seat." When she finally sees her husband for the first time in thirty years, his presence reduces her to silence. He directly asks her why she has tracked him down, but all she can do is "open and shut her mouth without any words coming out," like a puppet. Only once in the entire exchange between her husband, her sister, and herself does she manage to say anything, and even then it is only the whispered, sorrowfully pliant question, "What about me?" Ironically, her loss of language is the deciding factor in her husband's decision that she cannot fit into his American life. Speaking of the many guests he regularly entertains in his home, he says to Moon Orchid, "You can't talk to them. You can barely talk to me."

Any chance of a renewed personal relationship between Moon Orchid and her husband is doomed to fail because of the vast cultural differences between them. Moon Orchid's traditional Chinese upbringing has so completely conditioned her to be passive toward men, to accept unquestioningly any directive of her husband, that she cannot muster the emotional stamina needed to challenge his authority. "You don't have the hardness for this country," her husband tells her. He, however, does. He "smelled like an American," and he "looked directly at Moon Orchid the way the savages looked, looking for lies." He admits to Moon Orchid and her sister that he has "turned into a different person," and that they have become "people in a book I had read a long time ago." When Moon Orchid notes that her husband has lived in America for so long that he "talked like a child born here," she finally realizes that his power of language, which she does not have, is the greatest obstacle between them. This language difference, which symbolizes the diametrically opposed cultures in which each lives, never can be overcome. "Her husband looked like one of the ghosts passing the windows," Moon Orchid thinks, "and she must look like a ghost from China. They had indeed entered the land of ghosts, and they had become ghosts."

Following the dramatic meeting between Brave Orchid, Moon Orchid, and her husband in the car, Brave Orchid makes her brother-in-law take the two sisters to lunch, an odd, understated finale to the tumultuous conversation that has just occurred. Brave Orchid's son then drives his mother and aunt to Moon Orchid's daughter's home, where Moon Orchid will live. On the way, Brave Orchid tries to console her sister by minimizing the disastrous confrontation with Moon Orchid's husband. "Oh, well," she casually says. "We're all under the same sky and walk the same earth; we're alive together during the same moment." This theme of universality is remarkably similar to Kingston's own comforting comments to Brave Orchid at the end of the previous chapter.

Moon Orchid moves in with her daughter. However, as each day goes by, she becomes more emotionally disturbed and develops paranoid schizophrenia. She fears that "Mexican ghosts" are spying on her, and the one time that she talks on the phone to Brave Orchid, she quickly hangs up, saying, "They're listening. Hang up quickly before they trace you." She moves into an apartment of her own to escape the ghosts who are "plotting on her life" but eventually moves again, this time to Stockton to live with Brave Orchid, who tells Moon Orchid's daughter that she will cure her sister of this illness that is fear. To her own children, Brave Orchid explains their aunt's returning to live with them by expanding the talk-story about the emperor and his four wives: " . . . the wife who lost in battle was sent to the Northern Palace."

Living with Moon Orchid becomes more difficult day by day. She makes Brave Orchid's family turn off the lights and does not let them out of her sight. When Brave Orchid tells her family to humor her sister, the children hide in their rooms. Eventually, Moon Orchid starts to curse the family with bad omens, and Brave Orchid concedes that her sister has gone mad. Moon Orchid is institutionalized in an asylum, and soon thereafter she dies. Like No Name Woman, she "slipped away entirely," without proper identity and status.

Language again plays an important role in Moon Orchid's demise here at the end of "At the Western Palace." Returning to live with Brave Orchid in Stockton, Moon Orchid assures her sister that she heard Mexican ghosts talking in English about her. When Brave Orchid points out that Moon Orchid does not understand English, her younger sister replies, "This time, miraculously, I understood. I decoded their speech. I penetrated the words and understood what was happening inside." Ironically, Moon Orchid's decoding and penetrating the Mexican ghosts' language is similar to what Kingston was forced to do while growing up and listening to her mother's talk-stories. Because Brave Orchid never explained how the talk-stories were relevant to Kingston's life, Kingston had to interpret their meanings. Unfortunately, because Moon Orchid does not understand English, her interpretation of the Mexicans' English is based wholly on the insecurity she feels having been summarily rejected by her husband and now living in what for her must be a foreign, barbaric country. As Brave Orchid notes, "Moon Orchid had misplaced herself, her spirit (her 'attention,' Brave Orchid called it) scattered over the world." Not even Brave Orchid, who calls her sister's name in hopes that Moon Orchid's spirit will return to her body, can help her sister regain her lost identity.

Only during her brief stay in the insane asylum, before she dies, does Moon Orchid regain a sense of identity through language. Speaking to Brave Orchid, she joyfully explains that she and the other female residents "understand one another here. We speak the same language, the very same. They understand me, and I understand them." For the first time since Moon Orchid emigrated from China, she feels a sense of community: "We are all women here."

Why Moon Orchid initially developed paranoid schizophrenia and then eventually died, even after regaining a sense of identity, if only a false one, is best explained by Brave Orchid. "The difference between mad people and sane people," she warns her children, "is that sane people have variety when they talk-story. Mad people have only one story that they talk over and over." During the period in which Moon Orchid became more and more schizophrenic, she was obsessed with only one talk-story, that of the "Mexican ghosts" who were trying to kill her. In the asylum, she "had a new story" about how the other female patients were her daughters, but this one talk-story was the only story on which she fixated. Kingston, on the other hand, seems to understand what Brave Orchid means about a variety of talk-stories, which empower her like they do her mother. She draws on many talk-stories for *The Woman Warrior*, and, more important, she incorporates them into her personal life as best she can.

Although "At the Western Palace" seems less of a talk-story than the previous chapters, Kingston is strengthened by recalling Moon Orchid's struggle to assimilate in America. At the chapter's end, Kingston writes, "Brave Orchid's daughters decided fiercely that they would never let men be unfaithful to them," and then she adds, tongue-in-cheek, "All her children made up their minds to major in science or mathematics." Ironically, because of this comical, almost flippant last sentence, we are left wondering if such a lesson is worth the great expense—Moon Orchid's life—that was paid for the daughters to learn what they did.

- **taro leaves**   leaves of the tuberous taro plant, used to wrap food.
- **krisses**   swords.
- **butcher's block**   a square or rectangular surface, usually made of wood, on which a butcher cuts meat.
- **runners**   long, narrow tablecloths.
- **Brigitte Bardot**   (b. 1934) French actress who became an international sex symbol after starring in *And God Created Women* (1956), and who has worked tirelessly as an animal-rights activist.
- **"I Am a Person of the Middle Nation"**   In Chinese, the word "China" can be translated as "Middle Nation." The ancient Chinese believed that they were located at the center of the known world.
- **benevolent associations**   also known as tongs, protective associations that grew out of Chinese immigrants' need for protection against criminal members of their own society, as well as to secure social and economic rights for immigrants in the United States.
- **sandalwood**   a grayish brown tree native to Asia, whose wood is often used in wood carving.
- **pandanus fronds**   the narrow, spiny leaves, used in weaving mats, from the palmlike pandanus tree.
- **serrated**   jagged-edged, like a saw's teeth.
- **burlap**   also known as hessian cloth, a resilient fabric used in making sacks.
- **gesticulating**   gesturing.
- **jade trees**   succulent plants, with fleshy water-retaining leaves, domestically grown either in pots or in gardens.
- **"the bus with the mark of the dog on it"**   a Greyhound bus.
- **Thorazine**   the trademark name of chlorpromazine, an antipsychotic drug.

"A SONG FOR A BARBARIAN REED PIPE"

In this final chapter of *The Woman Warrior*, Kingston discusses further the difficulties she experienced growing up as a Chinese-American female. Greatest among these challenges was learning to speak English to non-Chinese people while struggling to confront traditional Chinese culture, represented by her mother, which inhibited her efforts to integrate fully into American culture. She searches to locate a middle ground in which she can live *within* each of these two respective cultures; while doing so, she creates a new, hybrid identity *between* them. At the close of the chapter, she draws on a talk-story about the legendary Chinese female poet Ts'ai Yen to demonstrate her own achievement of a delicate harmony between two competing cultures. Throughout her identity-forming process, she also finds that she must assert herself by breaking away emotionally from her mother, who has been the center of her life. Once free, she can develop an identity of her own.

"A Song for a Barbarian Reed Pipe" begins with Kingston admitting that she heard about Moon Orchid's disastrous confrontation with her husband, which Kingston related in "At the Western Palace," from her brother. She then amends this admission: "In fact, it wasn't me my brother told about going to Los Angeles; one of my sisters told me what he'd told her." This passing on of stories demonstrates the always-changing nature of talk-stories, whose telling is dependent on the teller. For example, Kingston recognizes that her brother narrates Moon Orchid's story differently than she. "His version of the story," she writes, "may be better than mine because of its bareness, not twisted into designs." However, she relishes her talk-stories' involved and complicated designs because they emphasize the complexity of both the talk-stories and, more important, their narrator—Kingston herself. Likening herself to a knot-maker who, long ago in China, would have continued to create a special, intricate knot even after the emperor banned its being made, Kingston tests the boundaries that her mother, Chinese culture, and American culture erect to manipulate her every thought and action.

Kingston follows the brief talk-story of the outlawed knot with a discussion between her mother and herself concerning Brave Orchid's supposedly cutting Kingston's frenum, the membrane under the tongue that restricts the tongue's movement. Although Kingston is unsure whether or not Brave Orchid truly sliced her frenum, she wants to believe that her mother did so as an act of empowerment: "Sometimes I felt very proud that my mother committed such a powerful act upon me." When Kingston again asks her mother why she cut Kingston's frenum, Brave Orchid's answer recalls the word "tied" from the talk-story about the Chinese knot-makers: "I cut it so that you would not be tongue-tied." Brave Orchid understands all too well the necessity of her daughter having the power of language, and the relationship between language and personal identity. Symbolically, Brave Orchid tells Kingston that she cut her frenum so that her tongue "would be able to move in any language. You'll be able to speak languages that are completely different from one another." Brave Orchid, a powerful Chinese woman in her own right, is concerned that Kingston succeed not only as a woman of Chinese descent but as a woman of Chinese descent living in America. In order to be successful, Kingston will have to learn to speak English, no matter how upsetting that is to the resigned Brave Orchid.

Kingston is confronted with her first challenge to speak English while attending kindergarten, but the fear and intimidation of publicly speaking English last well into her adulthood. Although she claims that she is making daily progress speaking English to strangers, she cannot forget her first three years of school, when her silence was "thickest." During these three years, she completely covered her school paintings with black paint, "layers of black over houses and flowers and suns." Concerned by these paintings, Kingston's teacher called her parents to the school, but they did not understand English and so could not discuss their daughter's behavior, other than Kingston's father cryptically telling Kingston that in China, "The parents and teachers of criminals were executed." To Kingston, however, these paintings represented the happy possibilities of curtains about to reveal "sunlight underneath, mighty operas."

Kingston enjoys being silent at school, but life becomes miserable when she eventually realizes that she is expected to speak. "At first it did not occur to me I was supposed to talk or to pass kindergarten," she writes, but when she flunks kindergarten, "silence became a misery." Compounding her misery is her feeling of being bad when she is supposed to speak and cannot. When she does speak, her voice comes out as a mere whisper. Ironically, her teacher's constantly instructing her to speak more loudly hinders rather than helps her confidence. Her fear of speaking recalls the previous chapter, in which Moon Orchid's ability to talk greatly diminished when she met her husband. The silence that Moon Orchid, Kingston, and other Chinese girls in Kingston's school experience seems culturally based. Moon Orchid never overcomes her apprehension to speak Chinese, her native language, to her husband; the adult Kingston still struggles to speak English publicly; and the Chinese schoolgirls, although they speak English sooner and more confidently than Kingston, are silent initially. "The other Chinese girls did not talk either," Kingston notes, "so I knew the silence had to do with being a Chinese girl."

The major obstacle to Kingston's learning to speak English is culturally based on the individual's relationship to society. Traditionally, Chinese custom frowns on a person, especially a female, who boldly and assertively speaks: Such behavior implies the individual's raised status over others. American culture, however, is theoretically based on the rights of individuals, not on the collective whole of society, and the English language, in which a subject—oftentimes the first-person, singular "I"—generally begins each sentence, reflects this cultural emphasis on individualism. But when Kingston, raised by parents who speak only Chinese, reads aloud in English, she stumbles constantly when saying "I." She writes, "I could not understand 'I.' The Chinese 'I' has seven strokes, intricacies. How could the American 'I,' assuredly wearing a hat like the Chinese, have only three strokes, the middle so straight?" Taught by her parents that proper behavior always means demurely acquiescing to others, she struggles with the defiant assertion of the self symbolized by the first-person, singular pronoun: "'I' is a capital and 'you' is lower-case." Also, like the word "here," "I" lacks strong consonants and has a "flat" sound, making it hard for a Chinese speaker to pronounce.

In contrast to spoken English, Chinese pronunciation appears hard and loud, or "chingchong ugly," as Kingston later characterizes it after she becomes more consciously attuned to American speech and values. This critical statement suggests her embarrassment at how she believes spoken Chinese sounds to American ears. However, cultural inhibition is not the only reason preventing the Chinese girls from speaking aloud. Rather, they want to be accepted as soft-spoken, American, and feminine. Ironically, although they think that they are being feminine, they are, in fact, being too soft to be heard.

Each day, following American school, the Chinese children go to Chinese school. There, the girls do not have the same silence problem that they do in the American school: They "screamed and yelled during recess" like everyone else. Reading Chinese aloud is not as difficult as reading English in the American public school because the children are not singled out to read before the entire class. All of the students read in unison: ". . . we chanted together, voices rising and falling, . . . everybody reading together, reciting together and not alone with one voice." However, the security that "together" affords Kingston is shattered when a new teacher arrives and makes individual students stand up and read aloud. This experience is too painful for the self-conscious Kingston and her sister, whose voices falter as regularly as they do in the American school: "When it was my turn," Kingston writes, "the same voice [as her sister's] came out, a crippled animal running on broken legs."

Kingston's and her sister's experiences in the Chinese school again emphasize language's power to create personal identities. Although we might expect Kingston to find comfort in speaking Chinese rather than English, she informs us that "you can't entrust your voice to the Chinese either; they want to capture your voice for their own use." For example, Brave Orchid forces Kingston, because she is older and speaks English better than the other family members, to demand "reparation candy" from a drugstore whose delivery boy mistakenly delivered medicine to Kingston's parents' laundry. Because Brave Orchid cannot speak English, she commandeers Kingston's voice to do her bidding and in the process embarrasses her daughter. "They want to fix up your tongue to speak for them," Kingston says of Chinese adults who refuse to learn English.

Even in the Chinese school, not all of the Chinese girls manage to speak. Kingston tells the story of one Chinese girl who is always silent. When this silent girl reads aloud in the classroom, she whispers, and no one ever hears her talk outside of class, not even on the Chinese school's playground. In the eyes of the other children, there is little difference between Kingston and this girl, and Kingston resents this public perception of her as being the same as the silent girl. She also recognizes the unpopularity and non-conformity in the girl's demeanor and fears that the girl's public image implies her own unpopularity and non-conformity. Kingston hates this silent girl.

One day, finding herself alone with the silent girl in the Chinese school's bathroom, Kingston confronts her and tries to make her talk. Despite becoming violent and brutal to her, Kingston cannot force the girl to talk; however, she does make her cry, although that was not Kingston's intention in confronting the girl. Ironically, by the end of this scene, Kingston finds *herself* crying alongside the silent girl. She finally recognizes that the girl is trying to deal with fears similar to her own. They are not so different after all. Following this episode, Kingston falls sick and spends eighteen months in bed at home. Her "mysterious illness," she believes, is retribution for her cruelty to the girl.

Ironically, Kingston's bullying and cajoling the silent girl to speak is yet another example of how people "want to capture your voice for their own use," although at the time, Kingston would not be aware of the hypocrisy of her own actions toward the girl. This episode, one of the few talk-stories not to originate from Brave Orchid, mirrors earlier stories in the novel in which females, language, silence, and identity are wholly and inextricably intertwined: No Name Woman's family's refusing to honor the memory of their suicidal relative, and Brave Orchid's subsuming Moon Orchid's voice within her own when the two women confront Moon Orchid's husband. "If you don't talk," Kingston explains to the silent girl, whom she never names and thus denies an identity to, much like No Name Woman's family denied *her* an identity, "you can't have a personality. . . . You've got to let people know you have a personality and a brain."

During her confrontation with the silent girl, Kingston's deep hatred of the girl lessens as she becomes more and more aware that she and the girl *are* alike: Both face similar fears inherent in assimilating into a new culture. Although Kingston resolves to make the silent girl speak, her inability to do so forces her to come to terms with her own fears associated with language and personal identity. At first, Kingston's voice is "steady and normal," but even after she physically hurts the silent girl by pulling her hair and pinching her skin and still the girl won't talk, Kingston begins losing control of her own emotions. She implores the girl to "Just say 'Stop,'" then screams "Talk" at the frightened girl, and then begs for any response: "You can even say 'a' or 'the,' and I'll let you go. Come on. Please." Finally, desperate and scared, she attempts to bribe her nemesis. "Look. I'll give you something if you talk," she pleads. "I'll give you my pencil box. I'll buy you some candy." Ironically, Kingston's offering candy to the silent girl recalls Brave Orchid's demanding "reparation candy" from the drugstore.

Kingston's lack of confidence in speaking English continues into adulthood, although she admits that English is easier to speak as she gets older. However, it remains painful for her to ask a bus driver for directions or even to say "hello" casually. "A telephone call makes my throat bleed and takes up that day's courage," she writes earlier in the chapter. Her difficulty in speaking English is mitigated by a feeling of shame about her Chinese culture and Chinese adults, who, from her Chinese-American perspective, appear unsophisticated—for example, her mother and her mother's generation still believe in ghosts and practice traditional Chinese customs.

Another reason for Kingston's anxiety about speaking English derives from her parents' mistrust of Americans, who, they suspect, will force them out of the country. Because of this deep-seated fear, Brave Orchid and her husband continually warn their children never to speak to American "ghosts": "There were secrets never to be said in front of the ghosts, immigration secrets whose telling could get us sent back to China." What Kingston's parents fail to recognize, however, is the precarious position in which they place their children, who are afraid to speak English for fear of entrapping their parents, but who are also mystified by the many secretive Chinese customs that Brave Orchid, who never explains her actions, performs. "Sometimes I hated the [American] ghosts for not letting us talk," Kingston writes; "sometimes I hated the secrecy of the Chinese. 'Don't tell,' said my parents, though we couldn't tell if we wanted to because we didn't know."

What complicates Kingston's divided loyalties between her parents' demanding that she not speak to Americans and her wanting to speak English to become more assimilated into American culture is her fear that "talking and not talking made the difference between sanity and insanity." She writes, "Insane people were the ones who couldn't explain themselves," which is precisely her predicament: She can't "explain" who she is because her parents order her not to, but she couldn't even if she wanted to because her parents refuse to tell her any *factual* information about their Chinese past, let alone the details of their coming to America. And what is even worse for Kingston are the many women she encounters who seem to support her belief that silence equals insanity. The "woman next door," who, we are led to believe, cannot conceive children, scares Kingston even though the woman "said nothing, did nothing"; Crazy Mary, who as a toddler was left behind in China by her parents when they immigrated to America, becomes insane because by the time she is reunited with her parents in America, Kingston infers, she is too old to master English; and Pee-A-Nah, "the village idiot, the public one," chases Kingston and her siblings, but not once does Kingston indicate that Pee-A-Nah actually *says* anything. Significantly, Kingston notes that the name "Pee-A-Nah," which one of Kingston's brothers made up, "does not have a meaning." Personal names are powerful words in that they represent our personal identities; however, a name that "does not have a meaning," that is indiscriminately used to identify a person, diminishes the unique individuality of that person. What frightens Kingston most is that *she* will become the village's next crazy woman, that *she* will be silenced like Crazy Mary and Pee-A-Nah and lose her emerging individuality.

To become more assimilated into American culture, Kingston believes that she must totally reject her "Chineseness," traits and customs that she connects most with her mother. She also decides that she will never be a slave or a wife, both female roles that she associates with Brave Orchid's talk-stories. When she suspects that her parents are planning to marry her off to one of the new Chinese emigrants, whom she refers to as "FOB's"—"Fresh-off-the-Boat's"— she displays behavior that she knows the suitor will find totally unacceptable in a traditional Chinese wife. Humorously, she writes, "I dropped two dishes . . . [and] limped across the floor. I twisted my mouth and caught my hand in the knots of my hair. I spilled soup on the FOB when I handed him his bowl." Because it was customary for the oldest daughter to be married before younger ones, Kingston knows that she can protect both herself and her sisters by being labeled an undesirable fool. By playing the fool, however, she plays a dangerous game, risking rejection from her Chinese society and being branded crazy—her biggest fear.

In addition to worrying about the newly arrived Chinese emigrants, Kingston becomes concerned when a Chinese boy starts visiting the family's laundry despite its always being hot and uncomfortable. When she realizes that this boy, whom she refers to as the "mentally retarded boy who followed me around, probably believing that we were two of a kind," visits the laundry because of her, she changes her work shift to avoid him. However, he figures out her new work schedule and continues to show up when she is working. Because her parents do not seem to mind the boy's visiting the laundry, Kingston suspects that they are matchmaking the two of them. She fears that the bumbling behavior she feigned to repel the "FOB's" is backfiring, and that her "undesirability" will lead her into a marriage with the boy: "I studied hard, got straight A's, but nobody seemed to see that I was smart and had nothing in common with this monster, this birth defect."

Kingston's belief that her parents are planning a wedding between her and the Chinese boy only compounds Kingston's fear that she really is as insane as Crazy Mary and Pee-A-Nah. She worries that she can so realistically imagine movies in her head, and that there are "adventurous people inside [her] head to whom [she] talked." When she no longer can keep her fears about her sanity to herself, she tries to tell one secret a day to her mother. Intentionally always talking to Brave Orchid when her mother is working late at night in the laundry, Kingston whispers her secrets to her mother, who only replies "Mm" and never stops working. One night, however, when Kingston "whispered and quacked" to let out another secret, Brave Orchid turns to her daughter and says, "I can't stand this whispering. . . . Senseless gabbings every night. I wish you would stop. Go away and work. Whispering, whispering, making no sense. Madness. I don't feel like hearing your craziness." Kingston is "relieved" that she can stop confessing to her mother, but Brave Orchid's comments about her daughter's "craziness" reinforce Kingston's fear that she might be insane: "I thought every house had to have its crazy woman or crazy girl, every village its idiot. Who would be It at our house? Probably me." She is, after all, the messy and clumsy one who had a "mysterious illness."

One day at the laundry, when the Chinese boy goes to the bathroom, Kingston's parents look inside the two mysterious cardboard crates that he always carries with him and find that the crates are full of pornography. To Kingston's amazement, Brave Orchid, rather than throwing the boy out of the laundry, only comments,

"My goodness, he's not too stupid to want to find out about women."

Kingston's isolation from and frustration with her parents, and especially Brave Orchid, who, Kingston feels, doesn't understand how badly her daughter wants an "American-normal" life, reach a climax after Brave Orchid's off-handed comment about the Chinese boy and his pornography. One evening, as the family sits eating dinner at the laundry, Kingston's "throat burst open," and out pours the many complaints she has been brooding over. She screams at her father and mother to tell the boy—"that hulk"—to leave the laundry and never come back. The boy leaves, never to be seen at the laundry again, but Kingston's outburst does not end there; she and Brave Orchid have a vehement shouting match.

Kingston shouts that she has her own future plans, which do not include marrying: She plans to apply for financial scholarships to colleges because her teachers say she is very smart. In effect, she rejects her Chinese life, which she perceives as holding her back from becoming Americanized, and prefers to leave Chinese school and run for a student office at her American school and join clubs. She blames Brave Orchid for not being able to teach her English, and, even more damning, she accuses her mother of confusing her with talk-stories. At the height of her emotions, she realizes that her long list of grievances is now "scrambled out of order," and that she is recalling things that occurred many years ago.

Symbolically, Kingston's list of complaints recalls the ideographs for revenge that Fa Mu Lan's father carved on the woman warrior's back in "White Tigers." In that chapter, Kingston noted that Fa Mu Lan's family's "list of grievances went on and on"; in "A Song for a Barbarian Reed Pipe," she writes, "I had grown inside me a list of over two hundred things that I had to tell my mother." Also, Kingston prays for a white horse—"white, the bad, mournful color"—like the "kingly white horse" that Fa Mu Lan rides into battle.

Kingston and Brave Orchid's argument ends with Brave Orchid shouting "Ho Chi Kuei"—"Ho Chi" means "like," and "Kuei" means "ghost"—at Kingston, who struggles to find meaning in the words. Chinese immigrants of Brave Orchid's generation frequently referred to their children as "Ho Chi Kuei," or half-ghosts, an expression that implies the Chinese-born immigrants' resentment of the American-born generation's rejecting traditional Chinese culture.

However, in an enigmatic and contradictory way, "Ho Chi Kuei" also suggests the older generation's jealousy—even pride—that their children can assimilate into American culture and prosper with relative ease. To Brave Orchid, Kingston has become "Ho Chi Kuei," or like a ghost-foreigner.

Although Brave Orchid, in her anger, threatens to kick Kingston out of the house, we are unsure if Kingston moves out immediately following the fight or later. However, while neither woman seems to win the argument, their relationship changes forever because each reveals closely held secrets. For example, when Kingston accuses Brave Orchid of always calling her ugly, Brave Orchid explains that the phrase is meant to *protect* Kingston, not harm her: "I didn't say you were ugly. . . . That's what we're supposed to say. That's what Chinese say. We like to say the opposite." Although Kingston does not fully understand that it is customary for Chinese parents to deny compliments paid to their children out of fear that vengeful gods might harm the children if the compliments are received vainly, she perceives that Brave Orchid is hurt by having to acknowledge her secret: "It seemed to hurt her to tell me that." She also discovers that Brave Orchid "cut" Kingston's frenum because Brave Orchid intended her daughter to "talk more, not less." And when Kingston accuses her mother of wanting to sell her as a slave, Brave Orchid, who argues that Kingston has misunderstood her all these years, retorts, "Who said we could sell you? We can't sell people. Can't you take a joke? You can't even tell a joke from real life."

Kingston's difficulty sorting what is factual in her life and what is imaginary continues even after she and Brave Orchid have their shouting match. For example, the phrase "Ho Chi Kuei" haunts her still, but she cannot ask anyone what this expression means: "I don't know any Chinese I can ask without getting myself scolded or teased, so I've been looking in books." However, she finds no definitive definition for the phrase, although she cynically remarks that one possible meaning is "dustpan-and-broom"—"a synonym for 'wife.'" Fearful of being ridiculed by Chinese people were she to ask them about Chinese customs she doesn't understand, Kingston searches for answers on her own but is unsuccessful. Consequently, she still cannot understand many of the things that Brave Orchid does—for example, placing drinks on the supper table for invisible ancestors. "I continue to sort out what's just my childhood, just my imagination, just my family, just the village, just movies, just living," she writes. "I had to leave home in order to see the world logically, logic the new way of seeing. . . . I enjoy the simplicity."

By confronting her mother, Kingston, for the first time in her life, discovers a strong, personal voice with which she can reconcile the competing Chinese and American cultures. She learns to exercise power over her world through the use of words and the ability to form ideas. Like Brave Orchid, she now can conquer her own ghosts using talk-stories. Apart from American ghosts, however, Chinese ghosts, particularly female ancestors and crazy women, still haunt her. Throughout the novel, the many women whom Kingston refers to, who commit suicide, are locked up, or even killed, suffer for their failure to find individualized voices that assert their selfhood. Similarly, Kingston, by asserting her identity—especially her *female* identity—through language, risks being branded "crazy" by her family and treated as an outcast, a "ghost," by the Chinese community.

Kingston introduces *The Woman Warrior*'s final talk-story, which focuses on the second-century Chinese female poet Ts'ai Yen, by saying, "Here is a story my mother told me, not when I was young, but recently, when I told her I also talk story. The beginning is hers, the ending, mine." Here, Kingston's choice of words is especially important: She publicly acknowledges that Brave Orchid's talk-stories still play a significant role in her life, and that she and Brave Orchid share a special bond between them—a love for talk-story.

The talk-story begins with Brave Orchid telling how Kingston's grandmother loved Chinese operas, and how her family, once while they attended an operatic performance, were almost hurt and robbed by bandits. Kingston then imagines that one of the operas her grandmother saw involved Ts'ai Yen, who is not as well known as the mythical Fa Mu Lan but whose life is better documented factually. Born in 177, not in 175 as Kingston suggests, Ts'ai Yen, the daughter of a wealthy scholar-statesman, was a musician and a poet. During a village raid in 195, she was captured by invading horsemen, whose chieftain made her his wife. For twelve years, she lived with these "barbarians" in the desert, and she even bore two children by the chieftain. Whenever the children's father would leave the family tent, Ts'ai Yen would talk and sing in

Chinese to her children. Eventually, she was ransomed and returned to her family so that she could remarry and produce Han—Chinese—descendants.

Among Ts'ai Yen's writings is the lamentation "Eighteen Stanzas for a Barbarian Reed Pipe," in which Ts'ai Yen relates her life among her captors and her return to her own people. The title of *The Woman Warrior*'s final chapter, based on Ts'ai Yen's title, suggests that Kingston identifies herself as living among "barbarians." More significant, however, is the symbolic relationship between Ts'ai Yen and Kingston's parents: Ts'ai Yen was physically forced to leave her village, and Kingston's parents, especially her father, because of depressed economic conditions in China, had no choice but to leave their homeland and seek employment in America; Ts'ai Yen characterizes her captors as barbarians, and Brave Orchid thinks all Americans are "barbarians"; and Ts'ai Yen, held captive for twelve years, sings about China and her Chinese family as a means to remember her cultural past; Brave Orchid's many talk-stories are her means of preserving her cultural past.

Although Ts'ai Yen eventually is reconciled with her family in China, Kingston only briefly notes the former captive's return to her homeland. Instead, she focuses on Ts'ai Yen's recognizing the validity of the barbarians' culture rather than on Ts'ai Yen's lamenting over her separation from her native culture. Because the barbarians and their culture symbolize Brave Orchid's perceptions of America, had Kingston dwelled on Ts'ai Yen's separation from her family and village while disparaging the nomads' culture, she would have validated the superiority, or supremacy, of a Chinese identity over an American identity; she would have justified Brave Orchid's belief that American culture is barbarous. However, by concentrating on Ts'ai Yen's recognition of and reconciliation with the nomads, Kingston suggests an ability to live harmoniously in both American and Chinese cultures. The talk-story implies not only Brave Orchid's recognition of American influences on her daughter, but also Kingston's own eventual acceptance of her Chinese past, which, after all, "translated well."

- **barbarian**   uncivilized and ignorant; the Chinese traditionally regarded all non-Han people as barbarians.

- **frenum**   here, a small fold of membrane that restrains the tongue's movement.
- **Chiang Kai-shek**   (1887–1975) leader of the Kuomintang, which means "national people's party"; in 1949, after three years of civil war, Chiang and the Nationalists were driven from mainland China by the Communists and established the Republic of China—in contrast to the Communist *People's* Republic of China—on the island of Taiwan, formerly known as Formosa.
- **teak**   an evergreen tree, native to southeast Asia, whose wood is used for furniture because of its durability.
- **tetherball**   a game in which two people try to hit a ball attached to the top of a pole by a rope until the rope is completely wound around the pole.
- **Korean War**   (1950–53) the military conflict fought on the Korean peninsula between northern Marxists, supported by the former Soviet Union, and southern Korean nationals, backed by the United States; following the conflict, the Korean Peninsula divided into North Korea and South Korea.
- **Cyclone fence**   a chain-link fence.
- **taps**   small metal discs attached to the soles of shoes, used to produce metallic sounds when tap-dancing.
- **cardigan**   a sweater that opens down the front.
- **cutworms**   larva that feed on plants, eventually cutting off a plant at ground level.
- **cannery**   a factory where food is canned.
- **fly screen**   a meshlike material used to keep flies out of homes or buildings.
- **wetbacks**   offensive slang, generally used to disparage people of Mexican descent who illegally enter the United States; here, Kingston means illegal Chinese immigrants.
- **Big Six**   meaning China.
- **Seagram's 7**   a brand of Canadian whiskey.
- **menses**   menstruation.
- **rictus**   a facial grimace.
- **camphoraceous**   musty-smelling; camphor, used both to soothe muscles and to repel insects, is produced by the camphor tree, an evergreen tree native to eastern Asia.

- **slough**   a depression in the ground, often muddy because of poor water drainage.
- **tules**   plants with grasslike leaves that grow in swamps and marshes.
- **cattails**   tall plants with flat leaves and elongated flowering spikes that grow best when rooted directly in water.
- **foxtails**   a perennial weedy grass with spiked flowers that resemble the tails of foxes.
- **dill**   a herb with aromatic leaves and seeds, which are used as a food seasoning.
- **chamomile**   a perennial herb with either yellow or white flowers; when dried, it is used to make herbal tea.
- **train trestle**   a bridge designed for trains to cross.
- **infanticide**   deliberately killing newborn infants.
- **second Communist five-year plan**   (1958–63) the economic program established by China's ruling Communist Party to spur the Chinese economy; this second five-year plan was marked by an experiment called the Great Leap Forward, which included a failed attempt to form agricultural communes, where peasants would live and work together to produce food for the entire country.
- **cudgel**   a club; here, a metaphor for a husband who beats his wife.
- **pestle**   a tool used for grinding or mashing food.
- **antiseptic**   sterile; non-threatening; not enlivening.
- **gaucheries**   rude, unmannered expressions.
- **bilingual**   the ability to speak more than one language fluently.
- **Southern Hsiung-nu**   a nomadic people who lived in present-day Siberia and Mongolia; the Hsiung-nu were especially powerful from the third century B.C. through the second century A.D., repeatedly making raids into northern China, which resulted in China's building the Great Wall.
- **desultorily**   lackadaisically, without fervor.
- **nock-whistles**   grooved whistles; the Hsiung-nu carved holes into their arrows; when shot, the arrows made whistling sounds because of the rush of air through the holes.

CRITICAL ESSAYS

THE THEME OF THE VOICELESS WOMAN IN *THE WOMAN WARRIOR*

Fundamental to *The Woman Warrior* is the theme of finding one's own, personal voice. Interspersed throughout the memoir's five chapters are numerous references to this physical and emotional struggle. For the many women who are voiceless, Kingston supplies the language these silent women need if they are to discover viable, individualized identities.

Beginning with the first chapter, "No Name Woman," Kingston breaks the family-imposed silence that surrounds the secret of an aunt, whom she names No Name Woman, who became pregnant by someone other than her husband. No Name Woman refuses to name the father of her child, protecting him with her silence, which simultaneously victimizes her: A nameless woman suggests someone with neither a story nor a voice. However, by hypothesizing how her aunt became pregnant, and by writing her aunt's story, Kingston in effect gives this silenced woman a voice. For Kingston, "the [aunt's] real punishment was not the raid swiftly inflicted by the villagers, but the family's deliberately forgetting her. . . . My aunt haunts me—her ghost drawn to me because now, after fifty years of neglect, I alone devote pages of paper to her." Although Kingston never learns what her aunt's real name was, the symbolic act of naming the woman No Name Woman honors this forgotten ancestor's memory.

If women do not have voices in traditional Chinese culture, then the talk-stories and legends that mothers pass on to daughters may indeed be considered subversive tales and instructions. One such talk-story, the legend of the Chinese woman warrior Fa Mu Lan, is a constant reminder to young Kingston that women can transcend socially imposed limitations. "White Tigers" is, in part, the story of Kingston's childhood fantasy of transcending a life of insignificance. As a child, Kingston imagines herself to be like Fa Mu Lan, who saves not only her family but her community. Brave Orchid's tale of this woman warrior exemplifies how talk-stories and legends create alternative, subversive voices for women who otherwise would remain silent their entire lives, dominated by a patriarchal world.

Kingston's young adult life, however, remains a voiceless one.

Juxtaposed with her fantasies of warrior grandeur in "White Tigers" are recollections of whispered protest at one of her employer's racist attitudes, which she challenges using a "small-person's voice that makes no impact." Refusing to type invitations for a different employer who chooses to hold a banquet at a restaurant being picketed by the National Association for the Advancement of Colored People and the Congress of Racial Equality, two political groups active in fighting racism, Kingston is immediately fired. But again her protest is whispered, her "voice unreliable."

Kingston's empowering women by creating individualized voices for them also extends to her own mother. Because Brave Orchid, despite her many years in America, does not speak English, she is effectively voiceless in her new world. Through Kingston, however, Brave Orchid's achievements are vocalized and recorded, as are all of the women's lives in *The Woman Warrior*. Kingston's memoir reveals Brave Orchid's sacrifices and lifts her out of the nameless Chinese crowd living in America. Ironically, however, this process of voicing women's experiences threatens Kingston's own self-esteem, especially in her relationship with her mother. For example, when a delivery boy mistakenly delivers pharmaceutical drugs to the family's laundry business, Brave Orchid is livid: Certainly, she thinks, the drugstore purposefully delivered the drugs to bring bad luck on her family. Brave Orchid forces Kingston, as the oldest child, to demand "reparation candy" from the druggist, a chore that Kingston finds embarrassing. "You can't entrust your voice to the Chinese, either," Kingston writes; "they want to capture your voice for their own use. They want to fix up your tongue to speak for them." In addition, Kingston's embarrassment stems from her perception that Chinese sounds "chingchong ugly" to Americans, like "guttural peasant noises."

Unfortunately, the personal cost of remaining silent, of *not* speaking "chingchong ugly" Chinese, is great, as Kingston's tale of Moon Orchid, her aunt, reveals. Moon Orchid's tragic story in "At the Western Palace" depicts a woman, deserted by her husband, who has so completely internalized the patriarchal view that women should always remain silent and never question male authority that she literally is silenced to death. The episode in which Moon Orchid reluctantly confronts her Americanized husband demonstrates how essentially voiceless a Chinese woman is who lives in a traditionally patriarchal society. Facing her husband after decades apart, Moon Orchid is unable to voice her years of rage and grief: "But all she did was open and shut her mouth without any words coming out." Later in the scene, Moon Orchid's husband explains to her, "I have important American guests who come inside my house to eat. . . . You can't talk to them. You can barely talk to me." Despite Moon Orchid's incessant talking in front of Brave Orchid's children, she is utterly mute while under the dominion of her husband. Ironically, even in the madness to which Moon Orchid succumbs after surviving her husband's emotional abuse, she is unable to talk. Again, Kingston, by writing Moon Orchid's story, puts the voice back into Moon Orchid's life.

In the memoir's last chapter, "A Song for a Barbarian Reed Pipe," Kingston relates her own search for a personal, individualized voice. If she finds that traditional Chinese society silences women, she also discovers that well-behaved females in American society are equally expected to be quiet. In order to feel even partially accepted in American culture, young Kingston retreats behind an emotional wall and loses her voice: "We American-Chinese girls had to whisper to make ourselves American-feminine. Apparently we whispered even more softly than the Americans. . . . Most of us eventually found some voice, however faltering." Despite this whispering, Kingston, even as a child, knows the consequences of being voiceless. In one poignant and painful episode, she describes the hatred she felt for another Chinese girl who refused to speak and the physical bullying she meted out to get this silent girl to talk. Ironically, her hatred for the girl is all the more vivid because this silent girl is so much like her—physically, emotionally, and socially. She fears becoming exactly like this voiceless (and nameless) girl, who serves as Kingston's alter ego.

In other aspects of her family life, Kingston feels the need to maintain a veil of secrecy. For example, because her parents came to the United States at a time when Chinese immigration was illegal, they and many other Chinese living in America kept a code of silence, a "never tell" policy regarding their cultural origins and history. However, this voicelessness further marginalizes Kingston and other first-generation Chinese Americans. For Kingston, writing *The Woman Warrior* is a cathartic and emotional experience, a form of therapy for herself and her family. Talking about her past becomes her cure for silence, her method of achieving an individual voice and a personal place as a Chinese-American woman in society.

THE WOMAN WARRIOR IN ITS HISTORICAL CONTEXT

In many ways, *The Woman Warrior* can best be understood in its historical context, particularly by three political incidents that occurred in the nineteenth and twentieth centuries: the Chinese May Fourth Movement of 1919, the Communist takeover of China in 1949, and, earlier, the Chinese Exclusion Act passed by the United States Congress in 1882. Although Kingston never directly discusses the May Fourth Movement or the Chinese Exclusion Act, and only indirectly the fallout from the Communists' assuming power in China, to a large degree the events in *The Woman Warrior* are influenced by these three historical circumstances.

Historians often mark the beginning of modern China and its literature with the May Fourth Movement of 1919. Originally a demonstration against Japanese expansionism into China, the protest rapidly coalesced into a political, social, and cultural movement that gave birth to China's Communist Party. On May 4, 1919, several thousand Chinese students gathered in Beijing's Tiananmen Square—the same square made famous in the West for the Chinese government-sanctioned 1989 student massacre—to protest the decision by the victorious Allies of World War I to cede Chinese territory to Japan. In the nineteenth century, Germany had won small territorial concessions from a weak China. Because Japan sided with the Western alliance against Germany in World War I, the Allies at the 1919 Versailles Peace Conference decided to give German-held territory in Shantung Province to Japan. When Chinese laborers, merchants, and others began supporting the student protest, the movement grew into a national crisis. The six-week standoff between the students and the Chinese government forced the Chinese delegation at the Versailles Peace Conference to reject the peace treaty.

The May Fourth Movement revolutionaries sought to replace China's heavy dependence on traditionalism with Western rationalism, democracy, and individualism. One of the cultural changes demanded by the activists, and one that has great consequences for modern Chinese literature, was the abandonment of classical Chinese, a language written but no longer spoken, in favor of a vernacular modern Chinese. The intellectuals wanted to adopt a written Chinese that was closer to colloquial Chinese, known as *baihua*. In support of this change, modern Chinese writers began adopting Western literary genres, including the novel, dramatic play, and short story. Writing for and about the general population, they created a new literary tradition using the spoken colloquial language, devoid of the sterile and overly stylized writing of ancient Chinese. Prominent in many of these new works are narratives using a first-person point of view, as well as themes of individualism and psychological self-examination.

This new literary and cultural movement influenced the attitudes of a new generation of Chinese. Because one of the cultural changes that the student demonstrators demanded was the education of women, in *The Woman Warrior*, Brave Orchid's decision to pursue a medical education must be understood in the context of the May Fourth Movement. Activists for educational change had been promoting universal education in China since the late nineteenth century, but many women remained uneducated even after 1919. Brave Orchid, who in 1934 graduated from medical college at the age of thirty-seven, is thus somewhat of a late beneficiary of this progressive change. Kingston recognizes the sacrifices that Brave Orchid made in first obtaining a medical education and then abandoning her career to join her husband in America. Simultaneously, however, Kingston is pained and marginalized by the traditional upbringing she experienced. Despite Brave Orchid's progressive education, in many ways Kingston's mother still remained a traditionalist.

The May Fourth Movement of 1919 also gave birth to the Chinese Communist Party. The Communists, who formally took over China in 1949 after a long armed struggle, soon began a program of purging landowners, whom they disparagingly labeled as capitalists, as well as anyone associated with the previous nationalist regime. Under communism, farmland was seized and redistributed among peasants, who spoke out against their former landlords and thereby were responsible for the Communist government's massacring anywhere from fifty thousand to several million former landowners.

Although Kingston discusses only briefly how the 1949 Communist takeover affected her relatives still living in China, the political problems these Chinese family members experienced certainly occurred during the period immediately following the governmental change of power. For example, in "White Tigers," Kingston recounts how in 1949, when she was nine years old, her parents received letters mailed from China that reported that Kingston's uncles "were made to kneel on broken glass during their trials and had confessed to being landowners." As such, they were executed. More gruesome is Kingston's account of the aunt "whose thumbs were twisted off." And the senseless killings of Kingston's relatives during the Communists' purge of landlords is best seen in the story of the uncle who is inhumanely slaughtered for "selfishly" capturing two doves to feed his family. Without allowing the man to defend his actions, the Communists trap him in a tree and then shoot him to death, "leaving his body in the tree as an example" to others.

A third political event that shapes Kingston's *The Woman Warrior* is the Chinese Exclusion Act of 1882, which was later followed by other anti-Chinese immigration laws in 1888, 1892, and 1924, all of which were passed into law by United States congresses intent on severely limiting the number of Chinese immigrants allowed into the country. In the nineteenth century, during the declining years of the Qing Dynasty (1644–1912), China experienced great famines, internal uprisings, and wars against Western powers. During this tumultuous period, many Chinese came to America to find work; they participated in the California gold rush and worked on the transcontinental railroad. Like European immigrants, the Chinese considered America, which they colloquially termed "Gold Mountain," a land of opportunities.

In the 1870s and 1880s, however, many Americans resented the presence of these Chinese immigrants, whom they saw as cheap labor and, therefore, an economic threat. These protectionist Americans pressured Congress to pass the 1882 Chinese Exclusion Act, which specifically restricted most Chinese from entering the United States and prevented those who were already in the country from gaining citizenship. To discourage the Chinese men who were already in the country from settling down and forming families, the act also barred Chinese women from entering the United States. In addition, anti-miscegenation laws prevented Chinese men from marrying non-Chinese women. As a result of these exclusionary laws, many Chinese who came to the United States in the late nineteenth and early twentieth centuries did so illegally. As illegal aliens, they lived underground lives, used fake identification papers, never mentioned their immigration status to non-Chinese people, and always avoided immigration authorities and the police. The Chinese Exclusion Act was not repealed until 1943.

In *The Woman Warrior*, although Kingston does not explain how her parents arrived in the United States, at least one of them must have arrived illegally. In *China Men*, the companion volume to *The Woman Warrior*, Kingston describes how her father used fake identification papers to gain entry into America and then, fifteen years later, sent for his wife from China. And in *The Woman Warrior*'s last chapter, "A Song for a Barbarian Reed Pipe," in which Kingston discusses her childhood memories of talking about illegal stowaways arriving in San Francisco's Chinatown, Brave Orchid warns her daughter never to mention her parents' immigration status to anyone, lest they be deported. Not surprising, such a life of existing outside of mainstream America deeply affected Kingston and many Chinese immigrant families, whose enforced silence protected parents from being deported but psychologically and emotionally confused the children trying to assimilate into a new, foreign culture.

THE WOMAN WARRIOR IN THE CHINESE LITERARY CONTEXT

In *The Woman Warrior*, Kingston addresses many of the same themes and concerns found in modern and traditional Chinese literature. Comparing Kingston's work to other Chinese literary texts can enhance our understanding of her memoir. In addition to Ts'ai Yen, a figure from traditional Chinese literature and culture who plays a prominent—though brief—role in *The Woman Warrior*, issues surrounding women's roles are common themes in the literature of many major twentieth-century Chinese writers, including Shen Congwen and Ding Ling, both of whom were influenced by reading Western literature. These two Chinese authors write about the conflicts arising from modern women's determination to find fulfillment and prominent voices in a traditionally patriarchal culture. Although unlikely that Kingston, who is more comfortable with the English language than Chinese, consulted the stories written by Shen and Ding, their texts, which deal with situations and contain incidents similar to those in *The Woman Warrior*, lend cultural and historical credence and authenticity to many of the episodes in Kingston's memoir.

Many of the events depicted in *The Woman Warrior* appear in other Chinese works of literature. For example, the talk-story about No Name Woman is highly reminiscent of Shen Congwen's short story "Xiaoxiao." One of modern China's best-known male writers, Shen, who often writes about issues stemming from the clash between modern and traditional Chinese culture, wrote "Xiaoxiao" in 1929. In the short story, Xiaoxiao, although betrothed to a young boy by her family, who live in rural China, becomes pregnant by her lover, a young errant laborer. After her lover abandons her, Xiaoxiao runs away from her family to join the female students in town. For her, girls who attend school represent freedom, an entirely new and modern concept for Chinese women. However, her family catches her running away and discovers that she is pregnant. Staunch traditionalists who blindly accept patriarchal society's status quo, Xiaoxiao's family must decide between two traditional options available to disgraced families such as theirs, whose daughters break sexual taboos: either kill Xiaoxiao by drowning her, or sell her. Her uncle chooses to sell her, but no one will buy Xiaoxiao. Only after she gives birth to a boy—and *not* to a girl—is she somehow redeemed. "The whole family loved the baby," Shen writes. "As he was a boy, Xiaoxiao was not sold after all."

The death of Kingston's aunt, No Name Woman, supposedly occurred in the same decade in which Shen wrote "Xiaoxiao." Because the practice of killing or selling adulteresses was still common, Kingston's portrayal of No Name Woman's suicide is a believable account of what might have happened to her aunt. As in Shen's story of Xiaoxiao, Kingston emphasizes the gender-biased prejudice that her aunt faced: "Mothers who love their children take them along [in death]. It was probably a girl; there is some hope of forgiveness for boys." However, what Kingston does not consider, perhaps because to do so is too emotionally charged, is that her aunt's suicide may not have been suicide at all, but may have been murder, an option that Xiaoxiao's uncle seriously weighs for his niece. No Name Woman gives birth first before committing suicide to see whether the baby is a boy or girl, for a male child could perhaps save her life. Following Kingston's deduction that the baby is likely a girl, perhaps No Name Woman, by drowning herself instead of letting a lynch mob execute her, simply fulfills the inevitable. As Kingston explains, boys are valued over girls in Chinese culture; even today in rural China, the practice of killing girls at birth is not unknown.

Another Chinese author whose literary works deal with many of the issues featured in *The Woman Warrior* is Ding Ling. In many of her short stories, for example, "Miss Sophie's Diary" and "When I was in Xia Village," she details the conflicts experienced by young women who try to secure personal, individual voices and freedoms in a twentieth-century China still shackled by patriarchal traditions. Ding Ling patterned these stories after the experiences of people she knew, particularly her mother, who had an unusual, non-traditional career analogous to that of Kingston's mother's. When Ding Ling's father died, her mother, who was then thirty years old, enrolled in the Provincial First Girls' Normal School to prepare for a career as a teacher. In the moving story "Mother," Ding Ling writes about her mother's courage and determination to succeed as a woman in a male-dominated society. As it was indeed rare for adult women in early-twentieth-century China to pursue professional studies, both Kingston's and Ding Ling's mothers made extraordinary career decisions. When Ding Ling's mother completed her education, she started two schools in Changsha, the capital of Hunan Province, and young Ding Ling began her education there.

In *The Woman Warrior*, Kingston repeatedly asserts the importance of education, recognizing that Chinese society, although it deems education very important, does not value educating women as much as men. To be a writer, scholar, and poet in China is to be held in high regard. Thus, the decisions of Ding Ling's and Kingston's mothers to pursue an education are even more extraordinary given societal limitations. Clearly, Kingston believes education to be liberating for women. Her own decision to become an educator and writer must be seen in this context.

Given the respect that Kingston has for educators and storytellers like herself, it is not coincidental that she ends *The Woman Warrior* with the true story of Ts'ai Yen, the first and greatest female poet of ancient China. Captured by the Southern Hsiung-nu in 195, Ts'ai Yen lived among her kidnappers for twelve years but could never fully assimilate into their culture. To cope with her separation from her family and village, Ts'ai Yen wrote "Eighteen Stanzas for a Barbarian Reed Pipe," in which she tells of her captivity and her feelings of alienation among foreigners. Similarly, Kingston, in her memoir's last chapter, named for Ts'ai Yen's poem, strongly implies her parents' anguish living in America and, to a lesser degree, her own sense of herself as an alien among "barbarians." Brave Orchid's talk-stories are like the song that Ts'ai Yen sings, which the barbarians cannot understand: "Ts'ai Yen sang about China and her family there. Her words seemed to be Chinese, but the barbarians understood their sadness and anger." The voice that Ts'ai Yen uses is a foreign one, not fully intelligible to others; Brave Orchid's talk-stories mystify Kingston, who struggles to find a personal meaning, something useful, in them. Like both her mother and Ts'ai Yen, Kingston establishes herself as a storyteller and scholar, an act of defiance against a culture that limits women. Claiming a personal voice that is both anguished and bold, she stresses the alienation that she feels living and growing up in a foreign culture. If Kingston's childhood fantasy was to be like Fa Mu Lan, a woman warrior who saves her family from an evil baron, her adult aspiration is to be like Ts'ai Yen, a poet who exorcises her grief through art, thereby saving herself and, indirectly, her family as well.

REVIEW QUESTIONS AND ESSAY TOPICS

(1). Why does Kingston begin *The Woman Warrior* with her mother's admonishment, "You must not tell anyone"? What effect does Kingston establish with this ironic statement?

(2). The mother-daughter relationship in *The Woman Warrior* has been described as "bittersweet." To what extent do you agree with this view? How would you describe this relationship?

(3). Throughout *The Woman Warrior*, Kingston explores how her Chinese cultural history can be reconciled with her emerging sense of herself as an American. Is she successful in this endeavor? Support your answer with examples from the text.

(4). Discuss the conflict between individualism and community as Kingston presents it in her text. Which characters struggle to define themselves as individuals in a community-oriented society? Are they successful in claiming their personal voices?

(5). Define "talk-story." Give an example of a talk-story and discuss how it fits your definition.

(6). Discuss the theme of silence in *The Woman Warrior*. Are any men silenced in the text? If so, who, and why?

(7). If No Name Woman had had a baby boy rather than a baby girl, would she have committed suicide by drowning herself and the baby in her family's well? Why or why not?

(8). What are some of the similarities between Kingston and No Name Woman? What are some of their differences?

(9). What role does Fa Mu Lan play in *The Woman Warrior*? How is this mythological woman warrior integrated into Kingston's narrative?

(10). In "White Tigers," what is significant about the rabbit's immolating itself for Fa Mu Lan?

(11). Discuss the symbolism of Fa Mu Lan's father's carving words of revenge into his daughter's bared back. Why does Fa Mu Lan's father and not her mother carve the words?

(12). How does the image of dragons in "White Tigers" relate to Kingston? To Brave Orchid? To these two women's relationship?

(13). Brave Orchid downplays the importance of Kingston's academic successes at school. Why?

(14). Although *The Woman Warrior* is a serious treatment of a Chinese-American woman's assimilation into a foreign culture, many episodes in the book are humorous. Discuss one event in the book that you find funny. Why is this event funny? Is there also a serious aspect of the episode you chose? How does Kingston integrate comedy and seriousness into her text?

(15). Despite Kingston's use of the term "Memoirs" in her subtitle, many literary critics consider *The Woman Warrior* an autobiographical novel. Because most readers consider autobiographies to be non-fiction, is "autobiographical novel" an oxymoron? Can autobiographies contain fictitious elements? Why or why not?

(16). What is significant about the term "ghost" in Kingston's text?

(17). Why does Brave Orchid think that it is important that she tell her personal history to her daughter in "Shaman"?

(18). Discuss the role of infanticide—intentionally killing newborn babies—in the book.

(19). Why does Kingston fear that her parents want to sell her and her sisters as slaves?

(20). Are there any sympathetic males in Kingston's narrative? If so, who are they, and what function do they serve? If no, why not?

(21). In the last section of "Shaman," Brave Orchid and Kingston discuss why Kingston never visits her mother. What are some of the reasons that Kingston offers? Does Brave Orchid understand her daughter's reasons? Why is this episode significant in their relationship?

(22). What is meant by the phrase "Little Dog"?

(23). Discuss Brave Orchid's perceptions of time and China in "Shaman" and "At the Western Palace."

(24). Compare Brave Orchid and her sister Moon Orchid.

(25). Are Kingston and Moon Orchid at all alike? If so, how?

(26). Discuss Moon Orchid's estranged husband in terms of his American-ness. How does he fit Brave Orchid's definition of "ghost"?

(27). Moon Orchid's stay with Brave Orchid and her family exposes ever-present misunderstandings between Brave Orchid and her children, and Moon Orchid and her nieces and nephews. Are these misunderstandings due to cultural or generational differences, or both?

(28). Throughout *The Woman Warrior*, Kingston stresses how she wants to be "American-normal." What does this term mean? What qualities make a person "American-normal"?

(29). In "At the Western Palace," Brave Orchid comments, "The difference between mad people and sane people . . . is that sane people have variety when they talk-story. Mad people have only one story that they talk over and over." Discuss this quote in terms of Moon Orchid's story, especially the time she spends in the insane asylum with the many pregnant women.

(30). Compare Ts'ai Yen's song of lament at the end of "A Song for a Barbarian Reed Pipe" to Brave Orchid's many talk-stories. Do the lamentation and the talk-stories serve similar purposes for the two women?

(31). In "A Song for a Barbarian Reed Pipe," Kingston describes her childhood cruelty to a silent Chinese girl at school. Why does she consider this an important episode to present to readers?

(32). Discuss the symbolism of Brave Orchid's telling Kingston that she cut her frenum.

(33). How do Kingston's experiences in both the American school and the Chinese school emphasize language's power to create a personal identity?

(34). What is the significance of the Chinese boy who begins visiting Kingston at the family laundry? Why does her parents' finding pornography in the boy's possession increase Kingston's anger at her mother?

(35). In "Cultural Mis-Reading by American Reviewers," an essay published in *Asian and Western Writers in Dialogue: New*

Cultural Identities (1982), Kingston criticizes those critics who find her work exotic and foreign. She states, "*The Woman Warrior* is an American book. . . . Yet many reviewers do not see the American-ness of it, nor the fact of my own Americanness." What are some of the American elements in this work? Do you agree with Kingston's position?

(36). To what degree does the lack of a chronological order in *The Woman Warrior* help construct a more interesting and engaging narrative? Does this non-chronological plot detract from gaining a better understanding of Kingston's memoir? Why or why not?

(37). Compare *The Woman Warrior* with other literary texts written by women of color. What similarities does it share with works such as *Beloved, The Color Purple*, and *The Joy Luck Club*? What are some major differences?

SELECTED BIBLIOGRAPHY

BEGUM, KHANI. "Confirming the Place of 'The Other': Gender and Ethnic Identity in Maxine Hong Kingston's *The Woman Warrior*." *New Perspectives on Women and Comedy*. Ed. Regina Barreca. Philadelphia: Gordon and Breach, 1992. 143–56.

BOORMAN, HOWARD L., ed. *Biographical Dictionary of Republican China*. New York: Columbia University Press. 1967.

DING LING. *Miss Sophie's Diary and Other Stories*. Trans. W. J. F. Jenner. Beijing: Panda Books, 1985.

FONG, BOBBY. "Maxine Hong Kingston's Autobiographical Strategy in *The Woman Warrior*." *Biography* 12 (1989): 116–26.

FRYE, JOANNE S. "*The Woman Warrior*: Claiming Narrative Power, Recreating Female Selfhood." *Faith of a (Woman) Writer*. Eds. Alice Kessler Harris and William McBrien. Westport, Connecticut: Greenwood, 1988. 293–301.

GARNER, SHIRLEY NELSON. "Breaking Silence: *The Woman Warrior*." *The Intimate Critique: Autobiographical Literary Criticism*. Eds. Diane P. Freedman, Olivia Frey, and Frances Murphy Zauhar. Durham, North Carolina: Duke University Press, 1993. 117–25.

GOLDMAN, MARLENE. "Naming the Unspeakable: The Mapping of Female Identity in Maxine Hong Kingston's *The Woman Warrior*." *International Women's Writing: New Landscapes of Identity*. Eds. Anne E. Brown and Marjanne E. Gooze. Westport, Connecticut: Greenwood, 1995. 223–32.

ISLAS, ARTURO. "Maxine Hong Kingston." *Women Writers of the West Coast: Speaking of Their Lives and Careers*. Ed. Marilyn Yalom. Santa Barbara: Capra, 1983. 11–19.

JOHNSTON, SUE ANN. "Empowerment through Mythological Imaginings in *The Woman Warrior*." *Biography* 16 (1993): 136–46.

LIM, SHIRLEY GEOK-LIN, ed. *Approaches to Teaching Kingston's* The Woman Warrior. New York: Modern Language Association, 1991.

LIM, SHIRLEY GEOK-LIN, and AMY LING, eds. *Reading the Literature of Asian Americans*. Philadelphia: Temple University Press, 1992.

MELCHIOR, BONNIE. "A Marginal 'I': The Autobiographical Self Deconstructed in Maxine Hong Kingston's *The Woman Warrior*." *Biography* 17 (1994): 281–95.

MILLER, MARGARET. "Threads of Identity in Maxine Hong Kingston's *The Woman Warrior*." *Biography* 6 (1983): 13–33.

MYLAN, SHERYL A. "The Mother as Other: Orientalism in Maxine Hong Kingston's *The Woman Warrior*." *Women of Color: Mother-Daughter Relationships in 20th Century Literature*. Ed. Elizabeth Brown Guillory. Austin: University of Texas Press, 1996. 132–52.

NISHIME, LEILANA. "Engendering Genre: Gender and Nationalism in *China Men* and *The Woman Warrior*." *MELUS* 20 (1995): 67-82.

RABINE, LESLIE W. "No Lost Paradise: Social Gender and Symbolic Gender in the Writings of Maxine Hong Kingston." *Signs: Journal of Women in Culture and Society* 12 (1987): 471-92.

RABINOWITZ, PAULA. "Eccentric Memories: A Conversation with Maxine Hong Kingston." *Michigan Quarterly Review* 26 (1987): 177-87.

SATO, GAYLE K. FUJITA. "Ghosts as Chinese-American Constructs in Maxine Hong Kingston's *The Woman Warrior*." *Haunting the House of Fiction: Feminist Perspectives on Ghost Stories by American Women*. Eds. Lynette Carpenter and Wendy K. Kolmar. Knoxville: University of Tennessee Press, 1991. 193-214.

SHEN CONGWEN. *The Border Town and Other Stories*. Trans. Gladys Yang. Beijing: Panda Books, 1981.

SLEDGE, LINDA CHING. "Maxine Hong Kingston's *China Men*: The Family Historian as Epic Poet." *MELUS* 7 (1980): 3-22.

TUSMITH, BONNIE. "Literary Tricksterism: Maxine Hong Kingston's *The Woman Warrior: Memoirs of a Girlhood Among Ghosts*." *Anxious Power: Reading, Writing, and Ambivalence in Narrative by Women*. Eds. Carol J. Singley and Susan E. Sweeney. Albany: State University of New York Press, 1993. 279-94.

WANG, JENNIE. "The Myth of Kingston's 'No Name Woman': Making Contextual and Intertextual Connections in Teaching Asian American Literature." *College English Association Critic* 59 (1996): 21-32.

WONG, SAU-LING CYNTHIA. "Autobiography as Guided Chinatown Tour? Maxine Hong Kingston's *The Woman Warrior* and the Chinese-American Autobiographical Controversy." *Multicultural Autobiography: American Lives*. Ed. James Robert Payne. Knoxville: University of Tennessee Press, 1992. 248-79.